Propagating Australian Plants

Macadamia seedling with cotyledons still enclosed in the endosperm of the seed. *Macadamia* seed will germinate readily if kept on a moist surface

Propagating Australian Plants

Alec M. Blombery and Betty Maloney

Nature is one place where miracles not only happen, but happen all the time—Thomas Wolfe, American novelist

Kangaroo Press

Introduction

The propagation of plants dates back to the beginning of civilisation, when grains were first cultivated for food. Today, interest in the cultivation and propagation of Australian plants is rising as many more Australian gardeners turn to our native plants in place of exotic species.

Standard propagation techniques can be used for most Australian plants, under the conditions normally found in gardens. In the main it is a matter of selecting the right technique for the particular plant. Special procedures must be followed for some plants, but then so they must for some exotics as well!

Many separate societies encourage the growing of various Australian plants, orchids and ferns, but in this book we have tried to bring all these interests together, including aspects of propagation to encourage a wider interest in our flora, and the methods outlined can readily be applied to exotic species.

Chapters 1 to 4 are a simple introduction to the plant kingdom, while Chapters 5 to 9 deal with the various methods of propagation. Monotone paintings by Betty Maloney make it easier to understand what occurs during the various processes of propagation. Factors associated with different kinds of propagation are discussed, ranging from the optimum conditions required for successful seed collecting and germination to the special requirements of various native orchids, ferns and other plants.

We have covered many of the simpler methods of propagation, while drawing attention to some of the more advanced techniques developed by researchers to produce large numbers of plants by advanced technology. Although tissue culture and micropropagation require expensive equipment and expertise, many mysteries associated with these advanced techniques are explained.

The material included here is intended for students and workers in the field of horticulture, for school students and for anyone who is fascinated by the world of Australian plants. We hope it will encourage them in their endeavours to produce Australian natives by propagation, thus increasing the planting and restoration of our native flora.

We extend our thanks to all those who have helped with the project, in particular to our friend Peter Abell for his advice, helpful comments, photographs and innumerable discussions on the physiology of plant propagation.

To Betty's husband, Reg, we extend our sincere thanks for his patience, understanding and help in many ways.

A.M.B. & B.M. 1994

© Alec M. Blombery and Betty Maloney 1994

Reprinted in 1997
First published in 1994 by Kangaroo Press Pty Ltd
3 Whitehall Road Kenthurst NSW 2156 Australia
P.O. Box 6125 Dural Delivery Centre NSW 2158
Printed in Hong Kong through Colorcraft Ltd

ISBN 0 86417 613 9

Contents

Introduction 4
1. General Botanical Concepts 7
    Thallophytes 7
    Bryophytes 7
    Pteridophytes 7
    Spermatophytes 8
2. Parts of the Plant 10
    Roots 10
    Stem 12
    Leaves 20
    Flowers 21
3. Fertilisation 24
    Ferns and Fern Allies 24
    Cycads and Conifers 24
    Flowering Plants 25
    Artificial Pollination 26
4. Fruits and Seeds 27
    Fruits 27
    Seeds 28
5. Fruit and Seed Collecting 29
    Fern Sori 30
    Achenes and Cypselas 34
    Berries 37
    Capsules 38
    Drupes and Fleshy Fruit 43
    Follicles 44
    Legumes or Pods 48
    Nuts 51
    Schizocarps 52

Seed Storage 52
Seed Characteristics 53
Viability 55
Preparation of Seed for Sowing 56
6. Germinating Seeds 58
    Soil 58
    Seed Boxes 58
    Fine Seed 59
    Medium-sized Seeds 59
    Large Seeds 60
    Growing Seedlings 60
7. Vegetative Propagation 64
    Cuttings 64
    Plant Hormones or Auxins 70
    Layering 74
    Division 76
    Grafting 77
    Budding 84
8. Orchid Propagation 87
    Propagation from Seed 87
    Vegetative Propagation 92
9. Fern Propagation 105
    Propagation from Spores 105
    Germinating Spores 106
    Vegetative Propagation 107
Appendix – Planting Out 114
Glossary 116
Bibliography 119
Index 120

THALLOPHYTES

(diagrammatic)

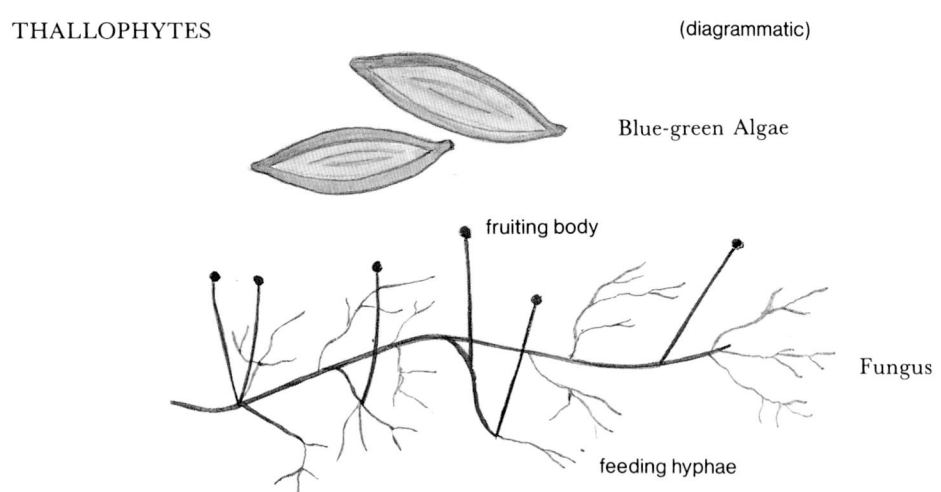

BRYOPHYTES

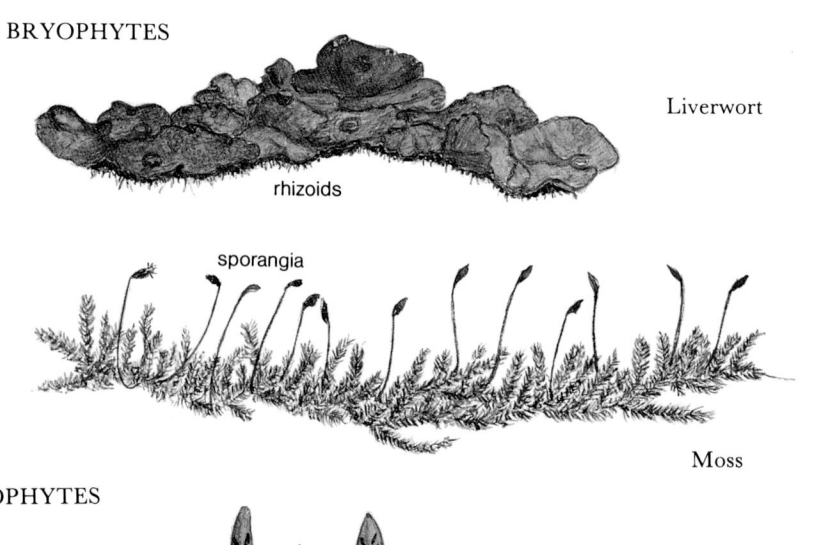

PTERIDOPHYTES

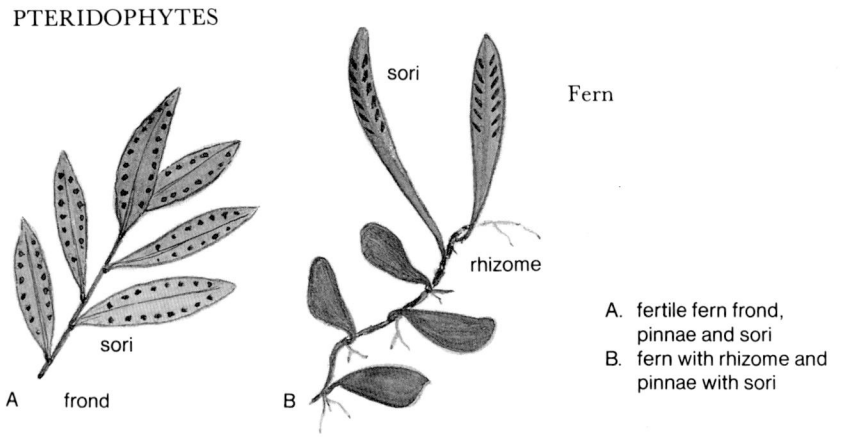

A. fertile fern frond, pinnae and sori
B. fern with rhizome and pinnae with sori

1 General Botanical Concepts

In this book the earlier, traditional system of classification of the plant kingdom is used, in which the plants are arranged in groups starting with the primitive types which have one or a few cells in their structure and finishing with the advanced flowering plants.

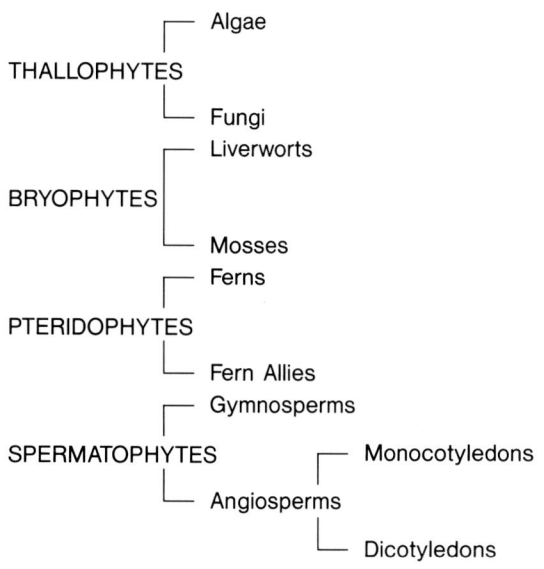

THALLOPHYTES

Algae and fungi are included in this group.

These are the plants of a single cell, or of one to many filaments which all appear similar. The vegetative part or body of these plants is called a thallus. There is no differentiation of the body of the plant into roots, stems and leaves.

Algae are simple plants that contain chlorophyll which may be masked by different pigments, such as brown pigment making brown algae, red pigment making red algae or blue pigment which with chlorophyll makes blue-green algae.

Fungi are thallophytes which do not contain chlorophyll.

This book is not concerned with the propagation of thallophytes.

BRYOPHYTES

Liverworts and mosses are included in this group.

The simple plants in this group have a vegetative thallus body like the thallophytes, which is differentiated into a green aerial body on which the sexual gametes unite for reproduction, and rhizoides, filamentous hair-like growths from the thallus which attach the plant to the surface on which it is growing.

Liverworts are bryophytes in which the green part of the body or thallus is entire or deeply lobed, often giving the appearance of having stem-like or leaf-like parts. They always have an upper and lower surface.

Mosses are bryophytes in which the green thallus or body is distinctly divided into leaf-like and stem-like parts. The stem-like section may or may not be branched. The leaf-like sections are arranged in a spiral pattern on the stem-like parts.

The propagation of bryophytes is not a concern of this work.

PTERIDOPHYTES

Pteridophytes are the ferns and fern-like allies which have true stems, leaves and roots. They are distinguished from bryophytes by their much greater complexity of tissue development, particularly in the distinct system of conductive or vascular vessels which connects the roots, stems and leaves. In the leaves the conductive system forms the veins. In many ferns the stem grows horizontally and is often underground. Sexual reproduction of these plants occurs by means of spores which are found in groups enclosed in a simple case or *sori*, located on the underside of a typical or modified fertile leaf or frond. Ferns also reproduce vegetatively by division of the rhizomes or by means of small adventitious plantlets which develop on the fronds of some species. See Chapter 9.

SPERMATOPHYTES
(Seed-bearing plants)

The more advanced seed-bearing plants, the spermatophytes, are divided into two groups; the non-flowering seed-bearing plants or gymnosperms, and the flowering seed-bearing plants or angiosperms. Their propagation is discussed at length.

GYMNOSPERMS

In gymnosperms the seeds are produced on the surface of scale-like leaves; they are known as naked seeds.

In cycads such as *Macrozamia, Lepidozamia, Bowenia* and *Cycas*, the male organs are spores carried on hard leaf-like scales called sporophylls, with a number forming a dense cone. The female organs are megasporophylls, hard leaf-like scales each bearing ovules. In *Macrozamia, Lepidozamia* and *Bowenia* these are carried on very short stalks around a central axis and form a dense cone, which may be very large. When ripe the cone breaks apart and the seed falls to the ground. In *Cycas* the megasporophylls have longer stalks and are arranged around a central axis which in the early stage of development appears cone-like; as the seeds develop the stalks of the megasporophylls increase in length and they become pendulous, forming a loose, long-stalked megasporophyll. In the pines *Araucaria* and *Callitris* a number of scale-like leaves form the cones. In the genus *Podocarpus* the male organs are grouped together in a slender cone, but the female organ appears singly and the seed is carried on a fleshy stalk resembling a small plum, which is often edible. The common name of Plum Pine is often applied to this genus.

ANGIOSPERMS

Angiosperms are the flowering plants, in which the seed is enclosed in a case regarded as a modified leaf, carpel or ovary, the female part of the flower. There may be one or a number of female organs or ovaries containing ovules which when fertilised develop into seeds.

The male organ of the flower is the stamen, which may or may not have a stalk called a filament. The male organ contains pollen, carried in a case known as an anther (part of the stamen).

In most plants the flowers have both male and female parts—these plants are called monoecious. In those species where the male and female parts occur on separate plants the plants are called dioecious.

When fertilised the ovules and ovary increase in size; together with the parts of the flower which remain attached when the seed is mature it is known as the fruit.

The angiosperms are further divided into dicotyledons and monocotyledons.

Dicotyledons

These plants have seeds with two cotyledons and their leaf venation is reticulate (in a network). Their vascular bundles of cells are arranged in cylinders on the outer part of the stem, concentrated in the cambium layer. The floral parts such as calyx, petals and stamens are chiefly in multiples of 4 or 5. The calyx and corolla are usually separate. The cambium layer may form woody annual growth rings.

Monocotyledons

These plants have seeds with one cotyledon. (Orchids are an exception: they have an embryo but no cotyledon.) The leaves have parallel veins and the vascular bundles are arranged throughout the stem tissue. With very few exceptions there is no cambium layer, no annual rings of wood are formed and there is no true bark, although a protective layer is formed on the outer surface of the stem. The stem consists of a considerable amount of spongy tissue and is frequently hollow. The floral parts are in groups of three and there is often no distinct calyx or corolla.

GENERAL BOTANICAL CONCEPTS

GYMNOSPERMS

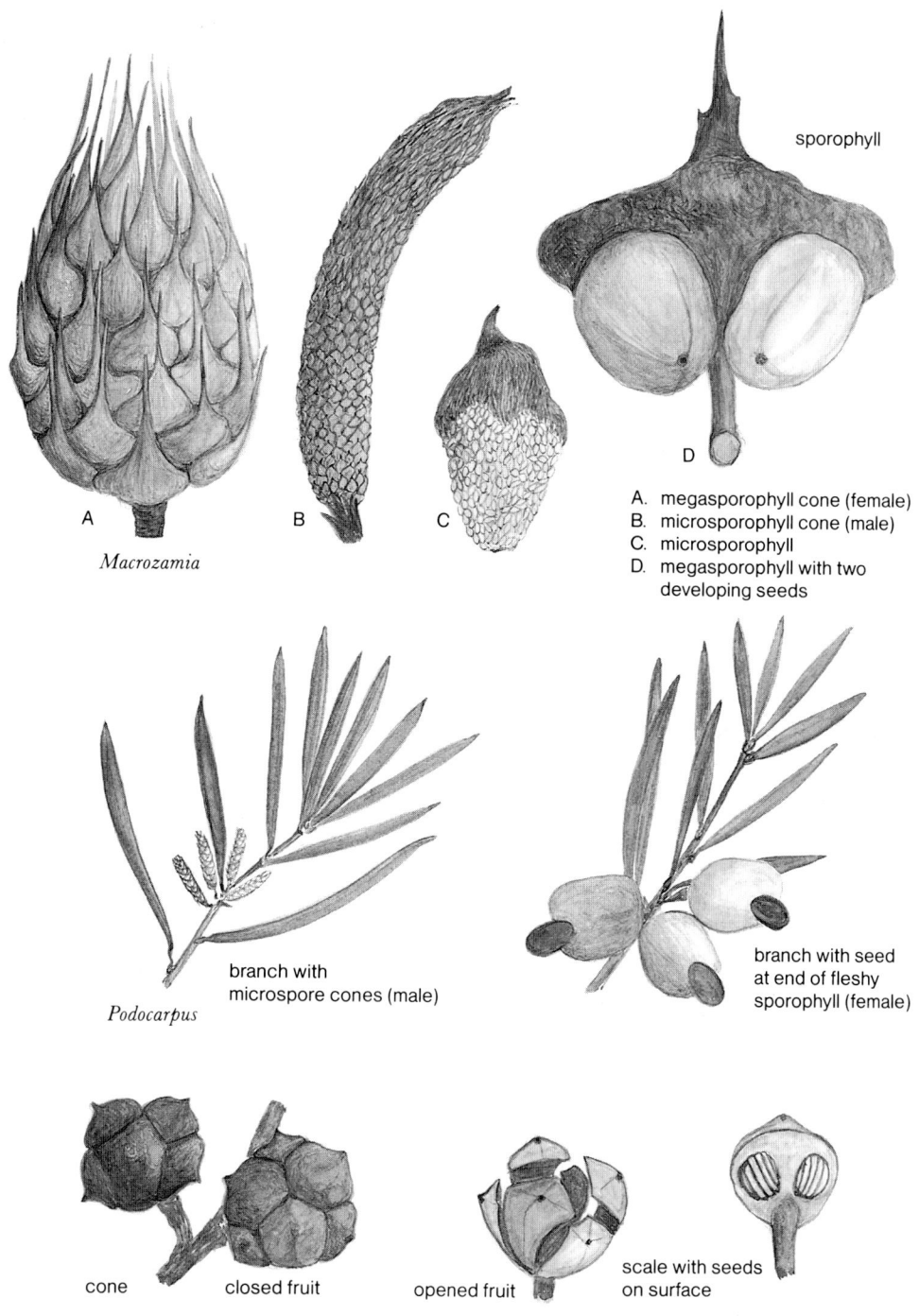

2 Parts of the Plant

To understand plant propagation more readily a knowledge of the parts of the plant is useful. The material in this section refers to the Pteridophytes (Ferns and Fern Allies) and the seed-bearing Gymnosperms and Angiosperms.

ROOTS

Roots hold the plant in the ground, or attach it to the surface of rocks or other plants (as in epiphytic orchids and ferns). The roots absorb moisture and substances including nitrogen, phosphorus and potassium and trace elements such as boron and copper. They may also store water and plant foods. In addition to the primary and secondary roots which develop from the radicle, plants are able to produce adventitious roots. These may arise from the stem, the branches or the leaves. Roots produce numerous minute hairs, estimated to number up to 19 per mm in some species, which enable the plant to absorb moisture and plant foods more readily.

Many plants have a symbiotic relationship with certain groups of fungi. A layer of fungi may enclose the root or grow into its tissues. When such fungi, known as mycorrhiza, are present there are few or no root hairs as the fungi provide the plant with water and other plant nutrients. In turn the plants provide the fungi with sugar and starches. This relationship between the root of the plant and the fungi is called symbiosis, and is of benefit to both. It has been estimated by some workers that up to 90% of plants may have a mycorrhizal association. Orchids have a mycorrhizal association essential to the germination of the seed, which have no cotyledons.

Some plants, like the Giant Lily, *Doryanthes*, have thick fleshy roots which store water; during dry periods they give up the water to the plant, contracting in the process and pulling the plant deeper into the ground. The inland Darling Lily, *Crinum flaccidum*, may have old bulbs up to a metre below the ground surface.

Some plants under certain conditions of stress develop aventitious stem buds from the roots. *Boronia pinnata*, for example, after being burnt by a bushfire, frequently develops adventitious shoots which grow into new plants, commonly called suckers, connected to the original plant. By carefully dividing the roots it is possible to transplant suckers and grow them on under nursery conditions as individual plants.

Where adventitious stem buds will develop, it is often possible to propagate new plants from pieces of roots with the aid of a suitable propagating medium.

Specialised Roots

Many species, in addition to those developing mycorrhiza, develop other specialised roots. In the pea family, Fabaceae, the roots develop bacterial nodules which are able to fix the nitrogen in the air into nitrogenous plant food.

Many of the family Proteaceae develop special roots which are able to absorb phosphorus efficiently, thus making use of the low phosphorus content in Australian soils. When fertilisers with a high phosphorus content are used, the specialised roots of most proteaceous plants absorb such large quantities that it becomes toxic to the plants.

Cycads develop specialised roots called coralloid roots in which beneficial specialised blue-green algae grow.

ROOT FORMS (diagrammatic)

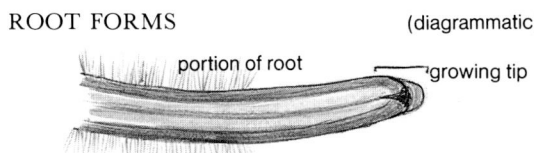
portion of root — growing tip — root hairs

section of roots with mycorrhiza

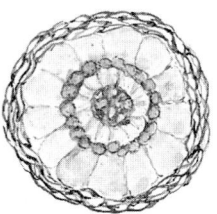
external ring of mycorrhiza (ectotrophic)

internal mycorrhiza (endotrophic)

root with bacterial nodules (rhizobia)

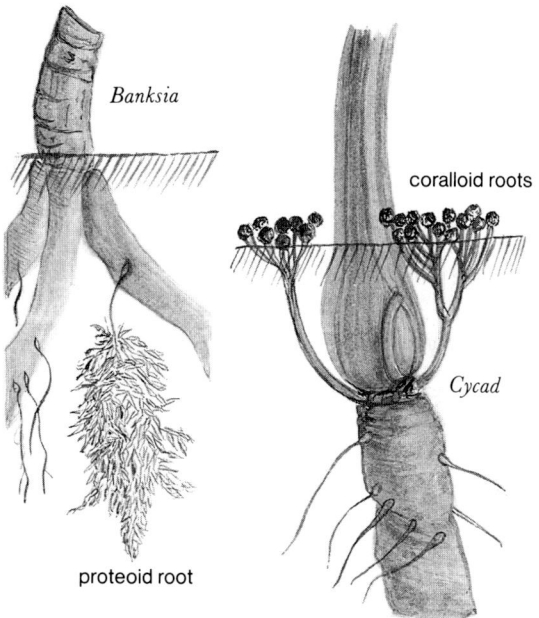
Banksia — proteoid root

Cycad — coralloid roots

STEM

The plant stem, which develops from the plumule of the seed embryo, has many forms. It may be erect, creeping, prostrate, above or below the ground, it may be twining, branched or unbranched (as in the majority of palms). In the orchid family it may be a fleshy and fibrous rhizome, from which pseudostems or pseudobulbs develop.

There is a considerable difference in the stem structure of monocotyledons and dicotyledons. In the former, except in very rare cases, there is no outer cambium layer and the vascular tissues which conduct water and plant food are scattered throughout the stem tissue. No annual ring of woody growth is produced and no true bark is formed, although a protective layer of cells is deposited on the outside of the stem. The stem increases in diameter by the deposition of cellular tissue. As a result of this stem structure, monocotyledons (with a few exceptions such as *Cordyline* and *Pleomele*) cannot be reproduced from sections of aerial stems. However, their underground stems or rhizomes, which have both bud shoots and adventitious roots, can be divided and propagated into new plants under nursery conditions.

Ferns, which have rather a primitive cell structure, can be vegetatively propagated from sections of rhizomes in a similar manner.

Many monocotyledons produce buds on the stem which may develop into branches or flowers.

In orchids adventitious growths frequently develop from dormant buds on the pseudostem and new plants form. These may be removed and grown on as separate plants.

When the stem of plants such as *Cordyline* is under stress, for example by being bent horizontally, adventitious growth may develop from a dormant bud, forming a new plant which may be removed and grown on.

In the case of tree ferns, the stem develops with masses of short roots, but apart from the apical growth does not produce bud shoots from the stem. The top section, if cut from the stem with its apical growth, may be developed as a separate plant under nursery conditions, although it may take one or two years before sufficient root growth has developed to support the plant. A constant supply of water is required over a long period for successful growth in the ground. As no further growth can develop from the lower section after the apical top has been removed, creating a new plant in this way results in the death of the parent.

Some plants have an underground stem or rhizome from which new aerial stems develop, but if the apical growth is removed the aerial stem dies as it has no dormant buds. Any damage to the aerial stem of a palm, which has no cambium layer, is permanent as no new tissue can be deposited to repair the damage as it can in dicotyledonous plants.

Exceptions to this rule are plants in the genus *Cycas*, which have a rather primitive cell structure; they are unusual in being able to produce new growth from the stem when the apical growth is damaged. Another unusual feature is that aerial roots may develop from a broken stem. In both cases it takes a number of years for this to occur.

The aerial stems of conifers and dicotyledons have the outer layer of tissue known as the cambium layer. This active growing part of the stem has numerous vascular tissue bundles, cambium tissue, phloem and xylem cells which lay down new plant tissue in an outer layer of woody tissue, forming annual rings. The cambium layer forms an outer layer of true bark which, as the plant becomes older, either thickens or may be continually shed as it develops.

An example of the variation of the bark is found in the genus *Eucalyptus*. In ironbarks the outer layer is hard and tough, in stringy barks fibrous and stringy, in bloodwoods scaly, in various other gums smooth. In older gums there may be a rough covering of bark at the base of the trunk.

Buds are produced from the nodes in the leaf axils, the upper junction between the leaf base and the stem. They may develop into new growth or remain dormant for an indefinite period. In eucalypts numerous dormant buds are produced on the stem. After a bushfire it is common to see new growth developing from the large trunk of the tree.

Other plants have dormant buds on a woody basal area known as a lignotuber; after destruction by fire or being cut back, new growths arise there—many Banksias, Telopeas and Lambertias do this.

Careful pruning can stimulate dormant buds into activity.

Many plants, particularly conifers, do not produce dormant buds on the stem. Such a plant scorched by fire may die.

PARTS OF THE PLANT

STEMS

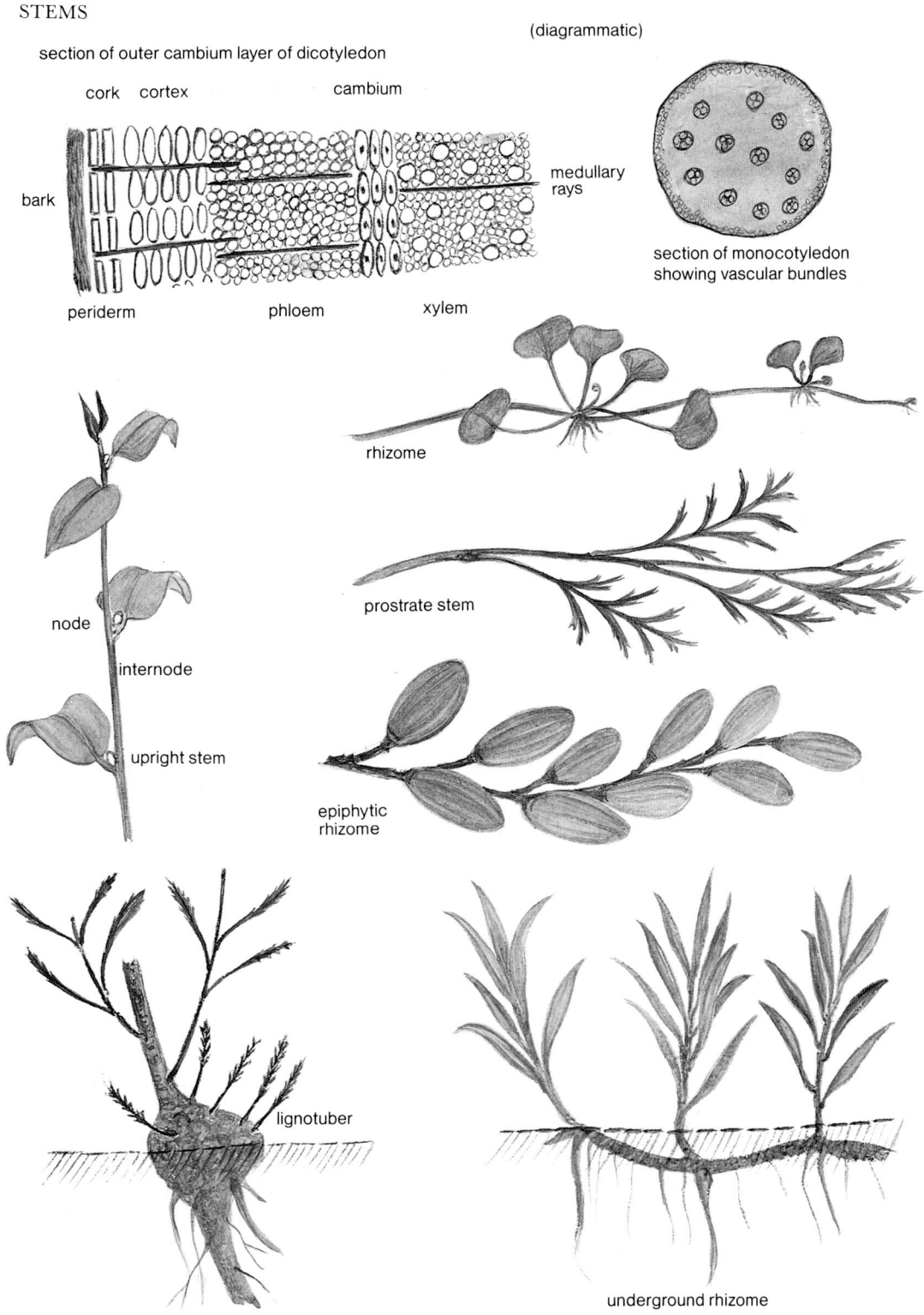

RHIZOMES

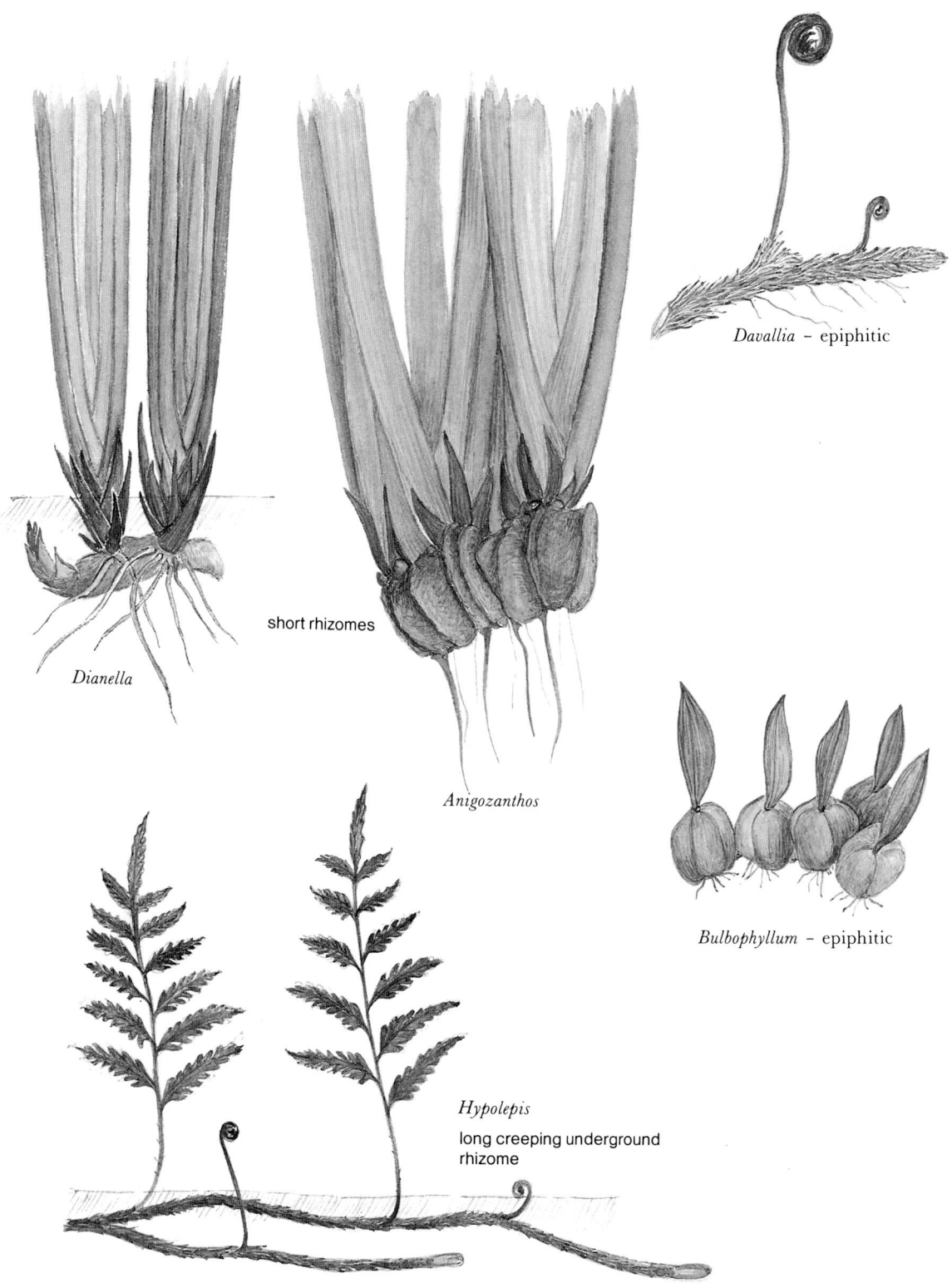

Rhizome

The less common stem, the underground stem known as a rhizome, may frequently be used for the purpose of vegetative propagation.

A rhizome is a creeping stem, often horizontal under or above the ground, found in many orchids and ferns, especially those which grow on the surface of rocks and plants. Rhizomes produce scale leaves which are often very small. As in aerial stems there is a node or shoot in the scale leaf axil which can develop into a new shoot; adventitious roots develop from the rhizome.

Plants with rhizomes can spread extensively. The rhizome may have short or long internodes and may form large dense clumps of aerial stems, as in *Dianella, Cordyline* and *Anigozanthos*, which have short underground rhizomes. Many ferns spread over wide areas by means of long underground rhizomes, e.g. bracken, *Pteridium esculentum*, Harsh Ground Fern, *Hypolepis muelleri*, and the Lacy Ground Fern, *Dennstaedtia davallioides*. Some have very short rhizomes and form clumps, e.g. the Broad Shield Fern, *Polystichum proliferum*. Other ferns with long creeping rhizomes which grow on the surface of rocks and trees are the Fragrant Fern, *Microsorium scandens*, and the Hare's-foot Fern, *Davallia pyxidata*.

In orchids the pseudobulbs or stems are very closely set on creeping rhizomes forming dense mats on rocks and the bark of suitable trees.

Plants which have rhizome growth are readily propagated. Sections of the rhizomes can be divided and grown under nursery conditions until established.

Doodia short creeping underground rhizome

Meristem Tissue

All new plant growth develops from a particular type of plant cell known as meristem tissue. Meristem tissue occurs in varying amounts throughout the growing parts of the plant, but is at its maximum in the growing tips of roots and shoots. In dicotyledonous plants the outer layer of the stem, the cambium layer, is rich in meristemic tissues. It is the presence of meristem tissue in the cambium layer which enables dicotyledonous plants to be propagated into new plants from pieces of the stem, and its absence in the aerial stems of monocotyledons (with a few exceptions such as *Cordyline*) which makes it impossible to propagate new plants from aerial stem cuttings, unless by the use of tissue culture. In *Cordyline* there is no cambium ring of cells, but secondary growth develops from meristemic zones around vascular bundles; the new growth does not form rings of wood as in dicotyledons.

Meristem tissue begins as undifferentiated cells which have the power, when acted upon by the plant's hormones, to differentiate into stem, leaf, root or flower tissue depending upon the plant's requirement.

Advances in plant technology have made use of meristem tissue to develop new plants. In tissue culture the growing tip is usually taken from a plant and the outer developing leaves removed, exposing the meristem tissue. Under specialised aseptic laboratory conditions the small piece of plant tissue is placed on a specially prepared medium with nutrients and hormone substances and manipulated to develop into plant tissue and finally small plants (known as cloning). The mass of growing tissue can be divided into smaller pieces and grown on in the prepared medium as before. This process can be repeated indefinitely, so that it is possible to produce an unlimited number of plants. It must be emphasised that considerable expertise and equipment is required for success.

In recent years there has been a change in the process—using special hormone substances the shoot, rather than growing into a separate plant, is encouraged to proliferate into a mass of small shoots. This mass of small shoots can be divided and planted on the growing medium. The process can be repeated endlessly until the required number of plants has been developed. The final plant masses are divided and placed on a different medium with rooting hormones; the small plants form roots and are ultimately divided into separate plants before being potted on under strict nursery conditions.

Many plants which are difficult to propagate are reproduced by this process of micropropagation.

PARTS OF THE PLANT   17

Above: *Lechenaultia*—Small plants proliferated from callus tissue

Anigozanthos—Microshoot on prepared medium ready to proliferate

Right: Small proliferating *Selaginella* plants from tissue culture callus *(Photo courtesy Peter Abell)*

Calostemma purpurea—Inflorescence arising from underground bulb with fruit forming

Blandfordia nobilis—Inflorescences arising from underground corms

Pterostylis curta—Leaves arising from multiple underground tuberoids

PARTS OF THE PLANT

BULB

The bulb is a short underground stem consisting of a central stem covered by overlapping scales, as in the culinary onion, *Allium*. Bulbs store food and water for the plant and produce new shoots and flowering stems. The bulb may remain underground or be partly above the surface. The roots of bulbs are usually thick and fleshy; during dry periods they give up their moisture and contract, drawing the bulb into the ground, as in *Crinum* and *Calostemma*. This type of plant is readily transplanted.

CORM

The corm is a very short underground stem with a thickened fleshy base and thin papery scale leaves, as in the exotic *Gladiolus*. The corms store food and water and may have several buds from which flower stems and new shoots develop. Examples of this kind of stem include *Blandfordia* and *Bulbine*. Older plants with several shoots may be divided and grown on under nursery conditions.

TUBER

The tuber consists of a swollen shoot or stem with a bud or buds capable of producing new plants. The domestic potato, *Solanum*, is a good example. In terrestial orchids such as *Acianthus, Caladenia* and *Pterostylis* the plants may develop a number of tubers, known as tuberoids, at the end of fleshy rhizomes. When the leaves of the orchid die down, the small tuberoids, which have a dormant bud, may be separated and grown as separate plants. Many species multiply under cultivation.

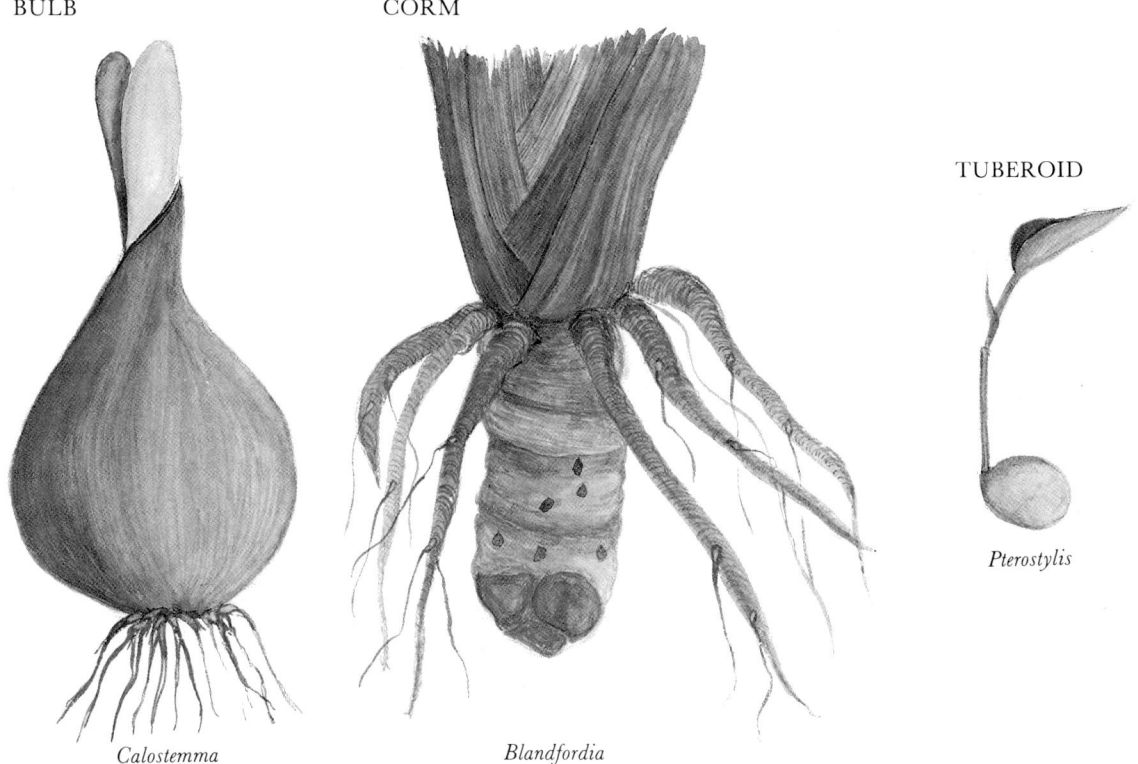

BULB — *Calostemma*

CORM — *Blandfordia*

TUBEROID — *Pterostylis*

LEAVES

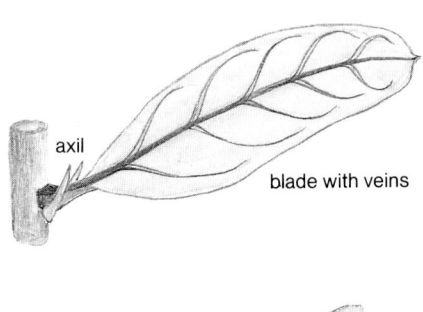
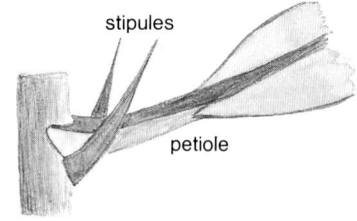
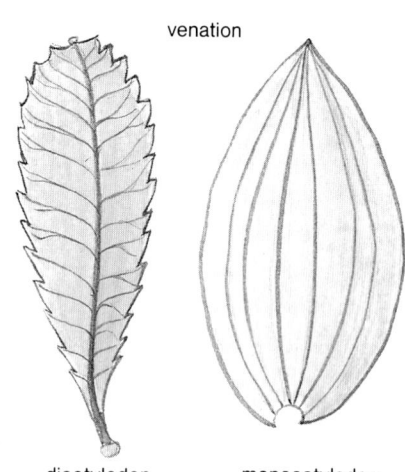
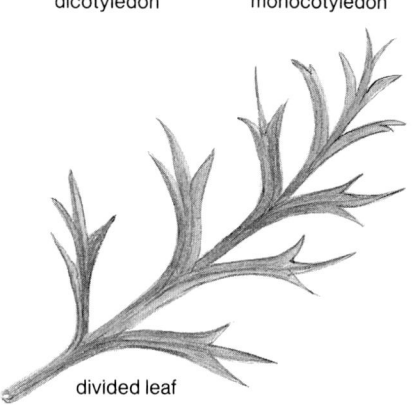

(diagrammatic)

A typical foliage leaf has an expanded section known as a blade. It has a number of ribs or veins, often called nerves, which support the soft portion of the leaf. The veins conduct sap to and from the leaves. The blade is joined to the stem by the petiole, a short or long stalk. When the stalk is absent the leaf is said to be sessile. The point where the leaf joins the stem is the axil, where there is often a pair of small scale-like, spiny or leafy outgrowths called stipules.

Leaves are distinguished from the stem by the absence of buds on the petiole and midrib. In some plants, e.g. in the family Geraniaceae (which includes the Australian tropical *Boea* and the African Violet), the leaves are able to form adventitious roots and buds when removed from the plant and placed on a propagating medium.

In dicotyledons there is usually a central vein or midrib and a network of branching veins.

In monocotyledons the veins are typically parallel to each other and merge together at the base of the leaf blade.

The leaf blade may be lobed or divided into a number of segments. Various forms of leaves may be scale-like, such as bracts, or modified for various purposes. The case or carpel of an ovary is regarded as a modified leaf. Floral parts are often regarded as modified leaves.

Phyllodes

When the leaf blade is absent, the stalk or petiole becomes flattened and serves the function of the leaf. This is known as a phyllode. Most *Acacia* have leaves reduced to phyllodes.

Stomata

Stomata are openings, usually on the undersides of leaves or their substitutes, which can open or close to allow gases and water vapour to enter or escape. Leaves give off moisture; to minimise the loss of water the leaves of Australian plants are often hairy, have a thick outer protective layer, are reduced in size or have become hard and spiny. In such plants as *Eucalyptus* the leaves may grow with the blade in a vertical position, turning the margin to the sun and thus reducing water loss.

Photosynthesis

A most important function of leaves and those parts containing green colouring matter is photosynthesis, a chemical process that occurs in the presence of light. When light falls on the green portions of plants the energy is absorbed by small particles in the cells known as chloroplasts which contain an assortment of pigments, one of which is chlorophyll, the substance chiefly responsible for the green colouring of plants. During photosynthesis carbon dioxide from the air, which enters the plant mainly by the leaves, is combined with water absorbed by the roots to form starches, sugars and oxygen. The sugars provide food for the plant and are also converted into the structural component of plant tissues and cellulose.

For a plant's proper functioning the moisture lost during transpiration and photosynthesis must be replaced. With cuttings this can be achieved in two ways:
1. By reducing the number of leaves. Unfortunately this reduces the cutting's ability to make new plant tissue and develop roots.
2. By growing the cuttings in a near saturated atmosphere. This is done by keeping the cuttings and medium moist in the confined space of cutting frames or a propagating house, by covering with plastic sheeting, a glass jar or plastic bag or by the provision of a constant supply of moisture by misting sprays. Unfortunately all these conditions are conducive to various fungal growths.

FLOWERS

The flower is the sexual reproductive part of the plant. The typical flower consists of a calyx, corolla, stamens and a pistil.

Calyx

The calyx consists of the outer series or whorl of floral leaves known as sepals. The sepals may be

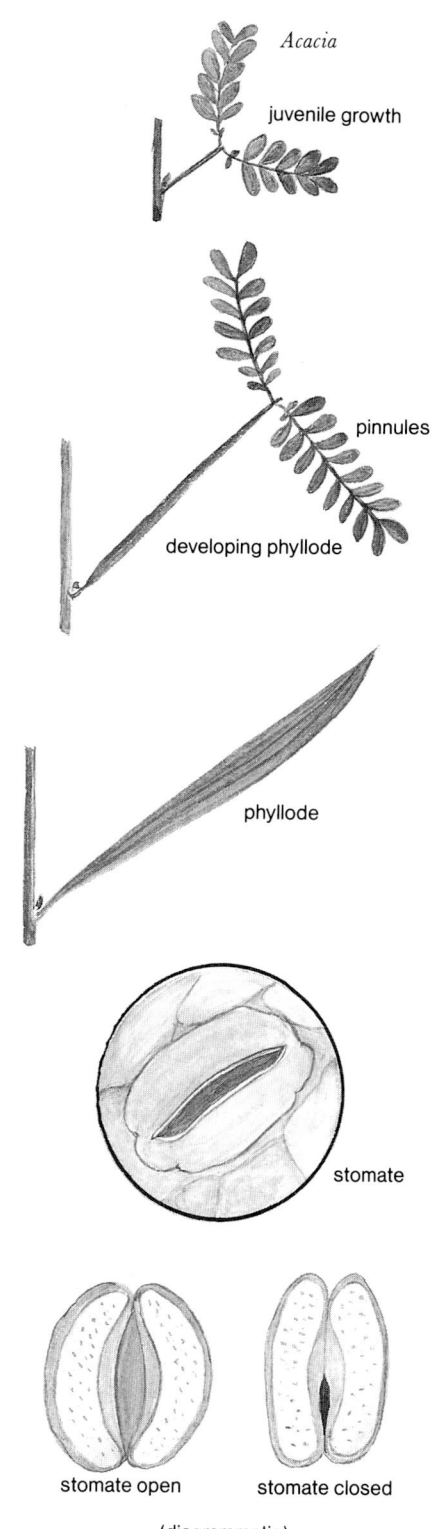

PARTS OF THE FLOWER

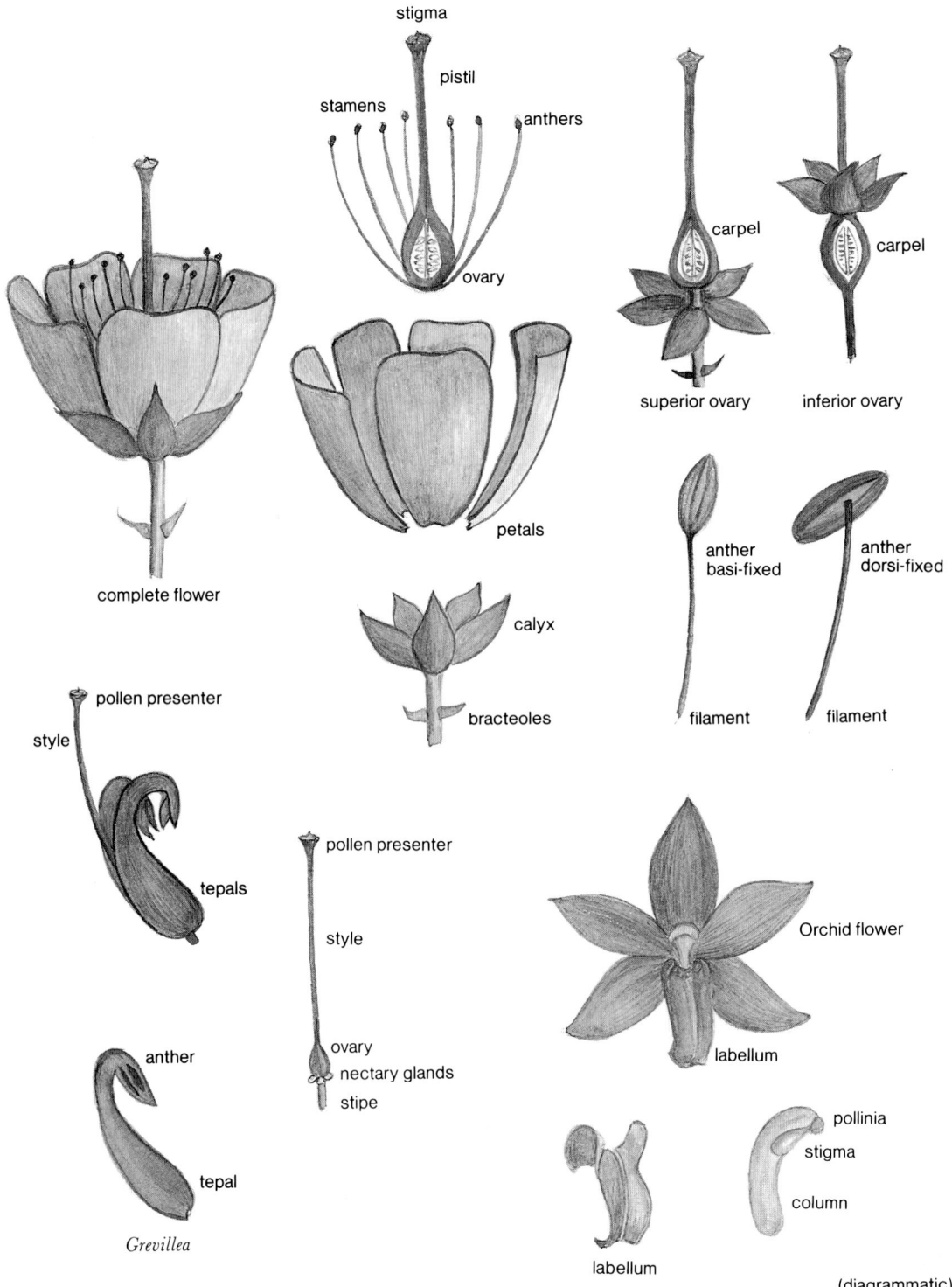

green and leaf-like, papery or petal-like (in plants such as *Thomasia* and *Brachychiton*). In some plants the sepals enlarge after fertilisation of the flowers and remain attached to the fruit, e.g. *Ceratopetalum* and *Clerodendron*.

In many monocotyledons and some dicotyledons the sepals and petals are indistinguishable and are known as tepals.

Corolla

The corolla is the inner whorl of floral leaves, each known as a petal. It may be large or small, usually coloured and attractive, or it may be absent in plants such as *Thomasia* and *Brachychiton*.

In orchids one petal may be greatly modified into a labellum which varies greatly in shape.

When the calyx and corolla are similar, as in *Grevillea*, it is called a perianth and each segment a tepal.

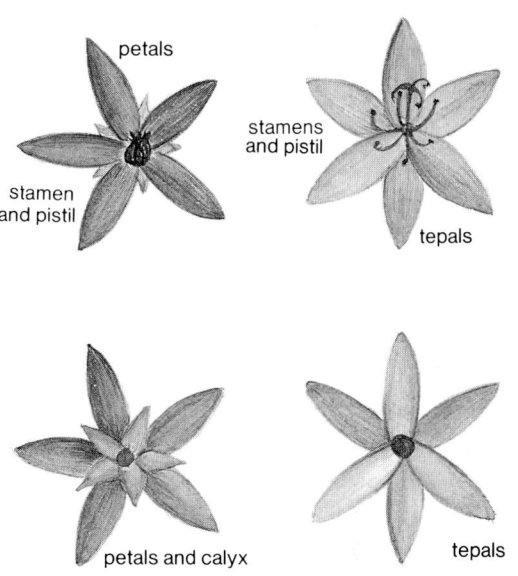

Stamens

The stamens are the male part of the flower. The anther containing the pollen is usually attached to a stalk or filament. When ripe the pollen is released from the anther. In the absence of a filament, the anther is sessile (attached directly to the floral parts).

In orchids the stamens are united with the pistil to form the column, the pollen masses at the apex being covered by a cap.

Pistil

The pistil is the female part of the flower. Its base is the ovary, which is a folded carpel forming a chamber in which there are a number of small eggs or ovules. When fertilised they form seeds. The ovary may have one or a number of separate chambers, each of which is known as a carpel. When the ovary is situated below the base of the calyx, it is called inferior; when it is above the calyx it is called superior; it may be part inferior or part superior. The style is a hollow tube connecting the ovary to the stigma and may be long or short. The stigma is at the apex of the style which may be entire or divided into lobes and is usually sticky to receive pollen.

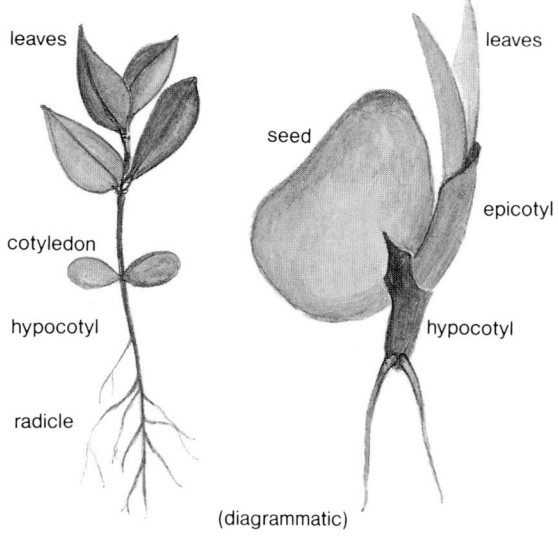

DICOTYLEDON   MONOCOTYLEDON

In orchids the pistil is combined with the stamens to form the column. The sticky stigma is below the pollen masses (pollinia) from which it is separated by a small outgrowth called a rostellum.

3 Fertilisation

Fertilisation is the union between male and female organs. The process differs in different types of plants.

FERNS AND FERN ALLIES

The development of new ferns occurs when ripe spores are released from the sori. When a spore reaches a favourable position it germinates into an intermediate stage, a tiny plant known as a prothallus. The female organs, archegonia, develop in the middle part of the prothallus while the male organs, antheridia, develop around the central portion. Each antheridium develops motile sperms which when ripe are released; providing sufficient moisture is present they swim through the moisture to an archegonium where they unite with the female egg cell. It is important when propagating ferns from spores to ensure that adequate moisture is always present.

CYCADS AND CONIFERS

In this group the pollen grains, when ripe, germinate into a male gametophyte before being shed. The male cells are carried by the wind to the micropyle of the developing female seed.

In cycads the developing seed gives out an exudate; the pollen grain sends out a pollen tube which is drawn into the micropyle by the exudate and unites with the egg cell, bringing about fertilisation. The seed at this stage is at an advanced stage of growth. When no pollen grain joins the seed it still develops but is infertile.

In cycads the pollen grain on entering the micropyle sends out a pollen tube to unite with the ovule and form a seed; it is usually retained for a period between the woody scales of the pine cone.

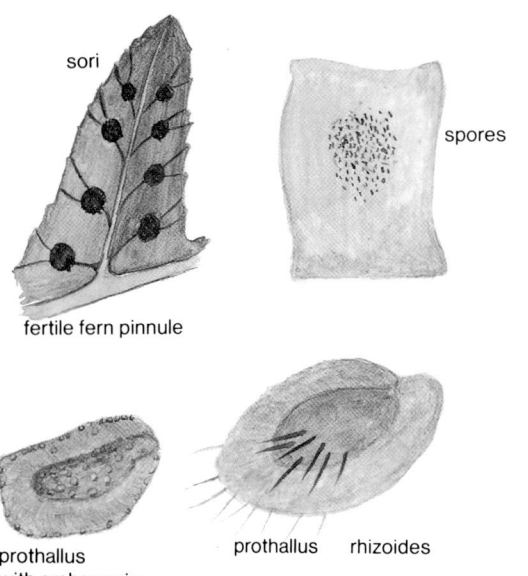

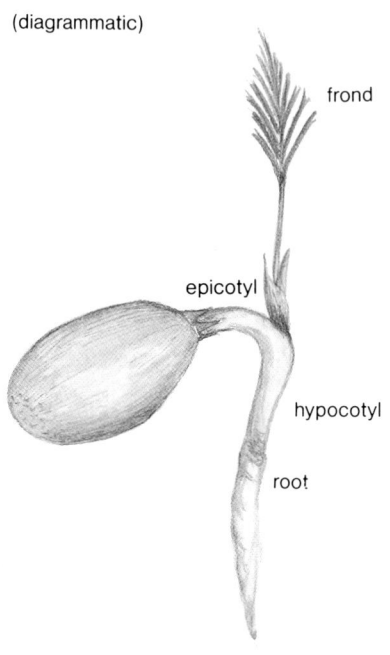

(diagrammatic)

Fertile germinating *Cycad* seed

FLOWERING PLANTS

In these plants the pollen grains when released from the anthers are carried by the wind, birds, insects or some other agency, and deposited on the stigma. If the stigma is receptive and the pollen ripe the pollen grain will germinate and produce a tube which grows through the stigma and down the hollow style until it reaches the ovary. If the egg cells are ripe, the tube unites with the ovule, fertilisation occurs and a seed develops. (In some species the receptive period is very short and fertilisation does not occur.)

Some plants are self-pollinating, as in the daisy family and orchids such as *Thelymitra*. When the flowers do not open but produce fertile seed, as in some species of Malvaceae, the plants are called cleistogamous.

In some species of *Banksia*, although there are thousands of flowers in an inflorescence, only a few flowers will develop seed—sometimes none.

Sometimes the ovary develops into a fruit which may not contain any seed or the testa may be present but contain no embryo.

In the family Proteaceae, particularly in the group Grevillioideae, the anthers are joined to the upper part of the tepals which in bud stage surrounds the end of the pistil. This pollen presenter has the stigma in the middle. When the pistil is released the pollen presenter is covered with pollen and until this is removed by some agent the stigma is not receptive to pollen from other flowers.

In many species of plants a large number of the seeds produced are infertile. This frequently accounts for the frustrating non-appearance of seedlings.

The length of time between fertilisation and the ripening of seeds varies with different species. With the daisies it may only be a few days but can be twelve months or more in the conifers *Agathus* and *Araucaria*. Seed commonly ripens in six weeks to four months, the period varying with weather conditions. Collecting the seed of any species thus depends on keeping the plant under observation.

Plants which release their seeds when ripe require especially close observation. They can appear green one day but may open the next. When only a few fruit have developed and there is doubt as to when the seed will be released a paper bag can be fastened over the fruit.

Seeds usually require a period to mature after their release from the plant, which varies from a few days to twelve months. Generally only a short period is required and many seeds lose their viability quickly. Correct storage is essential.

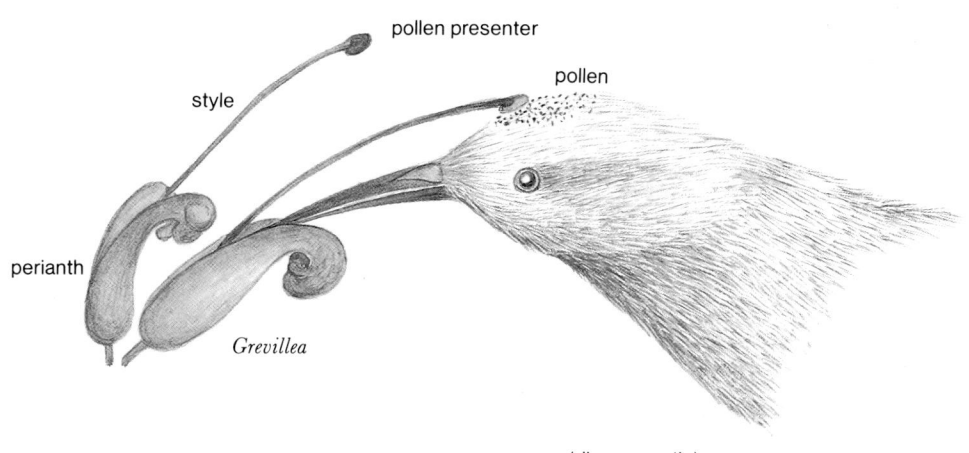

Cross-fertilisation by nectar-sipping bird

ARTIFICIAL POLLINATION

It is possible to increase the number of seeds from a particular plant by transferring the pollen manually (the method used to produce hybrids). Ripe pollen at this stage can be transferred to a receptive sticky stigma. A simple way to transfer pollen is with a small watercolour paint brush, picking it up from the open anther and transferring it to the sticky stigma of another flower. It is often necessary to repeat the operation a number of times to ensure that pollination occurs when the stigma is receptive, which may only be for a limited period, and that the pollen is fully ripe. To prevent cross-pollination by other agents cover the stigma with a small plastic bag. The best time to transfer pollen is when the flower is well developed.

In artificially pollinating an orchid a toothpick, or a match sharpened to a fine point, is used to transfer the pollen masses from the top of the column to the stigma just below the apex of the column.

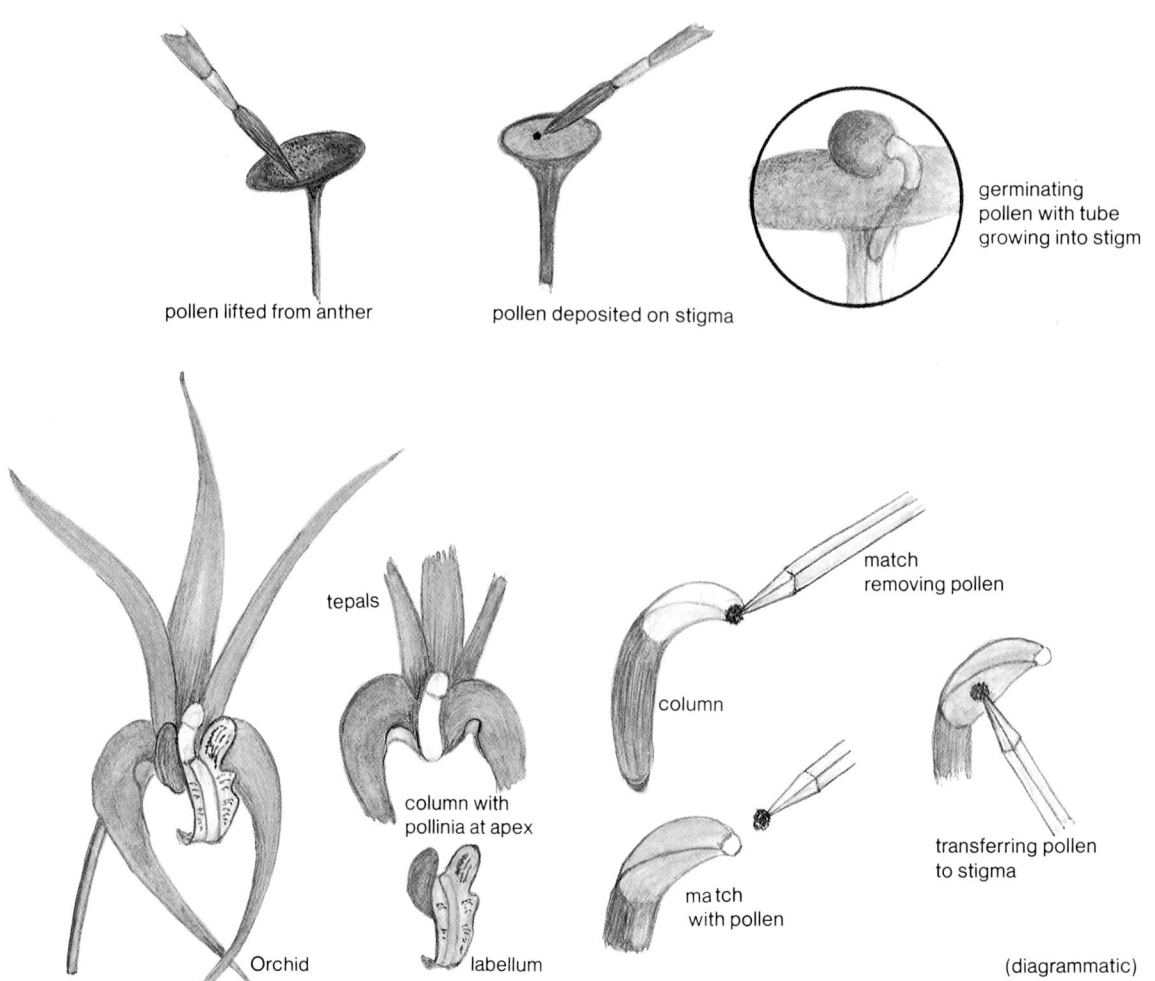

4 Fruits and Seeds

FRUITS

The fruit of a flowering plant consists of a ripened ovary with any growth which develops on the outer surface and any parts of the flower which remain attached. It may be dry or succulent or somewhere between the two, edible or inedible. The ovary may consist of a single chamber containing one or several seeds, or several chambers united into one large chamber. The fruit is said to be dehiscent if it splits open and releases the seed, indehiscent when it does not open.

ACHENE AND CYPSELA

An achene is a dry fruit formed from a superior ovary, which is indehiscent. It consists of a single carpel or chamber which contains one seed free of the ovary wall. The fruit of the daisy family is often referred to as an achene, but is believed by many authorities to be a cypsela, which is formed from an inferior ovary.

BERRY

A fleshy succulent indehiscent fruit, in which the seed is embedded in a fleshy layer.

CAPSULE

A dry dehiscent fruit consisting of two or more united carpels which may be soft or woody. In the Orchid family the capsule opens by splitting down the side. *Leptospermum, Eucalyptus, Isotoma* and *Wahlenbergia* capsules open by valves at the top, while *Tripladenia* (syn. *Kreysigia*) splits down the side.

DRUPE AND FLESHY FRUIT

A succulent fruit with an outer skin and a fleshy inner layer over a woody stony case which encloses the seed and is indehiscent, as in the common plum and *Persoonia*. Some fleshy fruit are drupaceous in appearance but are not botanically defined as drupes, e.g. *Syzygium*.

FOLLICLE

A dry dehiscent fruit formed from one carpel which may be thin to woody and first splits down one side as in *Grevillea, Telopea* and *Brachychiton*.

NUT

A dry indehiscent fruit with an outer shell containing one seed as in *Ceratopetalum*.

LEGUME OR POD

A dry dehiscent fruit which may split down one or two sides, as in the large family Fabaceae.

SCHIZOCARP

A dry dehiscent fruit which when ripe splits into a number of separate carpels, each called a mericarp or coccus and containing one seed, as in *Geranium, Prostanthera* and *Westringia*.

SEEDS

The seed consists of an embryo which has a central axis known as a hypocotyl, one or more cotyledons (absent in orchids), a radicle and a plumule.

Hypocotyl The hypocotyl is the central axis of the embryo to which the cotyledons are attached. The radicle is attached at one end of the hypocotyl and the plumule at the other end.

The hypocotyl plays an important part in the germination of the seed by increasing in length and thus drawing the radicle and plumule from the seed testa. It may raise the cotyledons above the soil or may extend outwards and downwards from the seed, when the seed body remains in or on the ground.

Cotyledons The cotyledons are the temporary seed leaves. They sometimes remain embedded in the endosperm, the food storage body of the seed. The cotyledons serve as a source of food and energy until the leaves and roots are able to supply the plant's requirements.

While monocotyledons have one cotyledon and dicotyledons have two, non-flowering plants such as cycads and conifers (pines) may have multiple cotyledons.

Orchids have no cotyledons and must depend in the natural state on a symbiotic relationship with particular types of fungi to obtain food and energy during germination. Under controlled germination the source of food is a special mix of nutrients in agar.

It is important when sowing seeds, particularly the finer types, not to sow them too deeply, as their available stored food and energy may be exhausted before the plumule reaches the surface. In contrast, in seeds from plants such as *Calostemma, Crinum,* various palms, cycads, pines and *Macadamia,* the cotyledons remain embedded in the seed endosperm. If they are broken away, the developing seedling either dies or grows very poorly.

Plumule The plumule is the embryo shoot from which the stem and leaves of the plant develop. When the plumule is broken off the hypocotyl no stem or leaves develop and the seedling generally dies. In rare cases an adventitious shoot may develop.

Radicle The roots develop from the radicle, at the opposite end of the hypocotyl to the plumule.

In conifers and cycads it is not uncommon for a root to develop from the radicle up to twelve months before the plumule develops.

The radicle frequently develops into a root even when broken.

Testa The testa is the external protective covering of the seed. It varies greatly in type, from thin and soft to hard and tough. It may have a water-repellant outer waxy coating.

The seed of some fruit may be enclosed in a woody case which does not open, e.g. *Macadamia,* or an inner woody case, which does not open and release seed, may enclose the seed inside a fleshy fruit, e.g. *Persoonia.*

Unless moisture can reach the embryo germination will not occur.

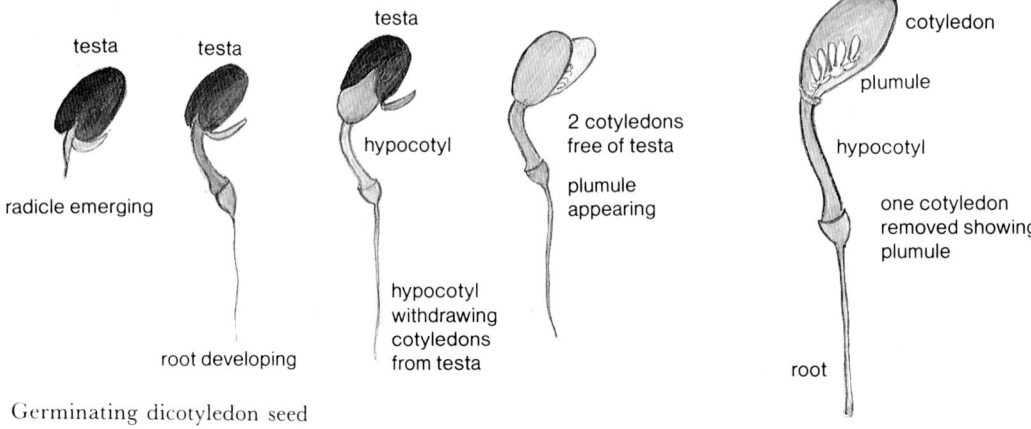

Germinating dicotyledon seed

5 Fruit and Seed Collecting

The ripening of seed is influenced by geographical location and climate. In the northern parts of Australia, seed may ripen two or three months earlier than in the southern regions. Seasonal conditions also influence flowering and ripening of seed.

Seed ripens much earlier in coastal areas than in elevated or inland areas. In mid-coastal New South Wales the seed of most late winter and spring flowering plants ripens between November and January. The waratah, *Telopea speciosissima*, gives an example of the influence of elevation: in the Sydney area the seed ripens about March, but in the elevated areas of the Blue Mountains it ripens between June and July.

The fruit of many plants develop slowly but when ripe may open and disperse their seed rapidly—that is, the fruit may appear green one day but open the following day, e.g. *Grevillea*.

The development of fruit and seed varies in different species. Some plants, e.g. daisies, develop fruit and seed within two or three weeks after flowering, while in other plants it may be between three and twelve months before fruit is ripe. So it is important that plants be kept under close observation.

When flowers fade the lower remaining section, which often includes the calyx, will slightly or markedly increase in size. Final growth of the fruit and ripening may be rapid.

There are three main seeding patterns.
1. Following fertilisation of the flower, the fruit and seed develop rapidly and when ripe release the seed. Some species retain seed for a limited period, e.g. eucalypts. Others release their seed slowly, e.g. *Brachychiton* and *Telopea*.
2. Fruit when ripe retain their seed for an indefinite period, usually until the branch or plant dies. Often the intense heat of a bushfire will cause the fruit to open and release the seed.

Just to make the seed-collector's life more difficult, some plants in genera which as a rule retain the seed shed their seed when ripe, e.g. *Banksia integrifolia, Callistemon acuminatus, Leptospermum laevigatum* and *Melaleuca leucadendron*.
3. Fruit containing the seed fall from the plant when ripe. Frequently such fruit do not open and release the seed, e.g. *Persoonia*, and the fleshy layer must be cleaned from the seed case for germination to occur.

Callistemon fruit

FERN SORI

Spores are the means of sexual reproduction in ferns. The spores develop in specialised cells known as sporangia. The sporangia are grouped together in sori, often enclosed in an outgrowth from the fern frond called an indusium. The sori occur on the underside of fertile fronds which often have a different appearance to infertile fronds. In the case of *Marsillea* the spore cases are independent of the barren fronds, and occur from the rhizome at the base of the frond.

Pyrrosia

Grammitis

Nephrolepis

Pellaea

Microsorium

Dictymia

Fern Sori

The sori are arranged differently in each genus of ferns. They may be arranged along the veins either singly or in clusters, they may be arranged in rows or they may cover the undersurface of the frond. The sori may also occur singly or in clusters along the leaflet margins or in continuous rows along the margins, or in a row on the top edge of the margin.

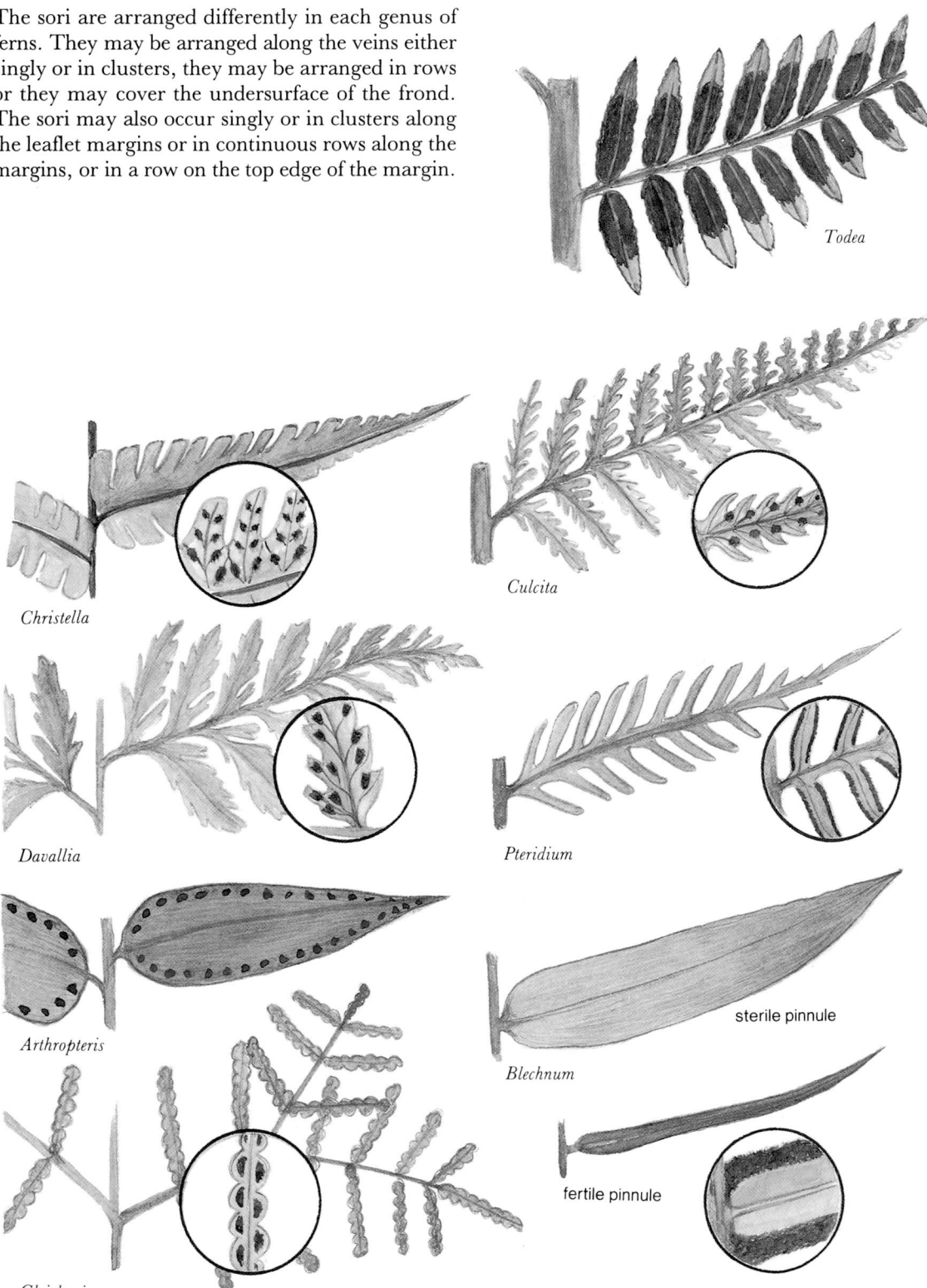

Fern Sori

Sori may also appear as a continuous mass on the lower side of the frond, with a felt-like appearance. This mass may be attacked by the larva of a small beetle which destroys the felt-like sori spores, covering it with frass (fine dusty excrement).

To determine whether the spores are ripe gently tap or scrape the undersurface of the frond. Dust-like spores will fall if they are mature.

Platycerium

Lindsaea

Adiantum

Asplenium australasicum
(Bird's Nest Fern)

FRUIT AND SEED COLLECTING   33

Fern Sori

To collect the spores from a fertile frond place a section inside a folded sheet of paper. The dust-like spores, if ripe, should dehisce within a few days. If no spores appear after a week or two, keep the fern under observation until the spores are ripe.

Sow the spores immediately or store them temporarily in a jar or paper envelope. Spores lose their viability quickly, so it is important to sow them soon after collection.

strobilus

Lycopodium
(pendulous)

strobilus

Lycopodium
(erect)

fronds

sporophylls

strobilus

Asplenium flabellifolium
(Necklace Fern)

Marsillea

Selaginella

ACHENES AND CYPSELAS

Seed can disperse quickly so close observation after flowering is needed to ensure collection.

The dry indehiscent one-seeded fruit formed from a superior ovary are termed achenes, e.g. *Clematis* and *Ranunculus*.

In *Clematis* clusters of ripe fruit with fluffy appendages give a bearded appearance, while in *Ranunculus* the fruit is a head of achenes each with a beak from a persistent style.

Indehiscent fruit formed from an inferior ovary are termed cypselas. They often have a persistent pappus or cluster of hairs, e.g. *Rodanthe* and *Craspedia*.

Craspedia *Bracteantha* *Olearia* *Brachycome* *Clematis* *Ranunculus*

FRUIT AND SEED COLLECTING 35

Ceratopetalum gummiferum Nut fruit with surrounding coloured calyx

Below left: *Cordyline stricta* berry fruit

Below: *Cordyline cannifolia* berry fruit

Emmenosperma alphitonioides with drupaceous fruit

Cycas armstrongii Plants with ripened seeds hanging from base of fronds

FRUIT AND SEED COLLECTING

BERRIES

The seeds embedded in the fleshy fruit of berries must be separated from the pulp before being stored.

Squeeze the berries and rinse them under the tap in a strainer to wash away the pulp. Dry thoroughly on paper before storing.

Berries generally change colour and become soft when ripe. In *Cordyline*, seed within the berry will sometimes germinate before falling.

Smilax

Solanum

Cordyline

CAPSULES

Capsule seed cases can be soft or woody and come in a variety of shapes and sizes.

Soft, urn-like capsules develop quickly after flowering in plants such as *Wahlenbergia* and *Stylidium*, and disperse their seed when ripe. Gather when the capsules begin to turn brown.

Hard woody capsules, which in some cases take twelve months to mature, remain on the plant for an indefinite time, e.g. *Callistemon, Leptospermum* and *Melaleuca*. Collect older fruiting spikes and secure

Orchid

Calostemma

Leptospermum

Baeckea

Melaleuca

Melaleuca

Stylidium

FRUIT AND SEED COLLECTING 39

in a paper bag until seed is released—generally in one or two weeks.

The long triangular capsule of *Blandfordia* grows out beyond the spent floral tube, dries and splits to release a number of seeds.

The *Hibiscus* fruit is an inflated five-celled capsule. Handle with care when it splits as there are frequently fine sharp irritating hairs among the seed.

Insects often destroy the seeds in the *Angophora* capsule, which contains three flat seeds, released when the valves open.

Gather mature unsplit capsules and store in paper bags until seeds are released.

Lophostemon

Angophora

Wahlenbergia   *Blandfordia*   *Hibiscus*   *Burchardia*

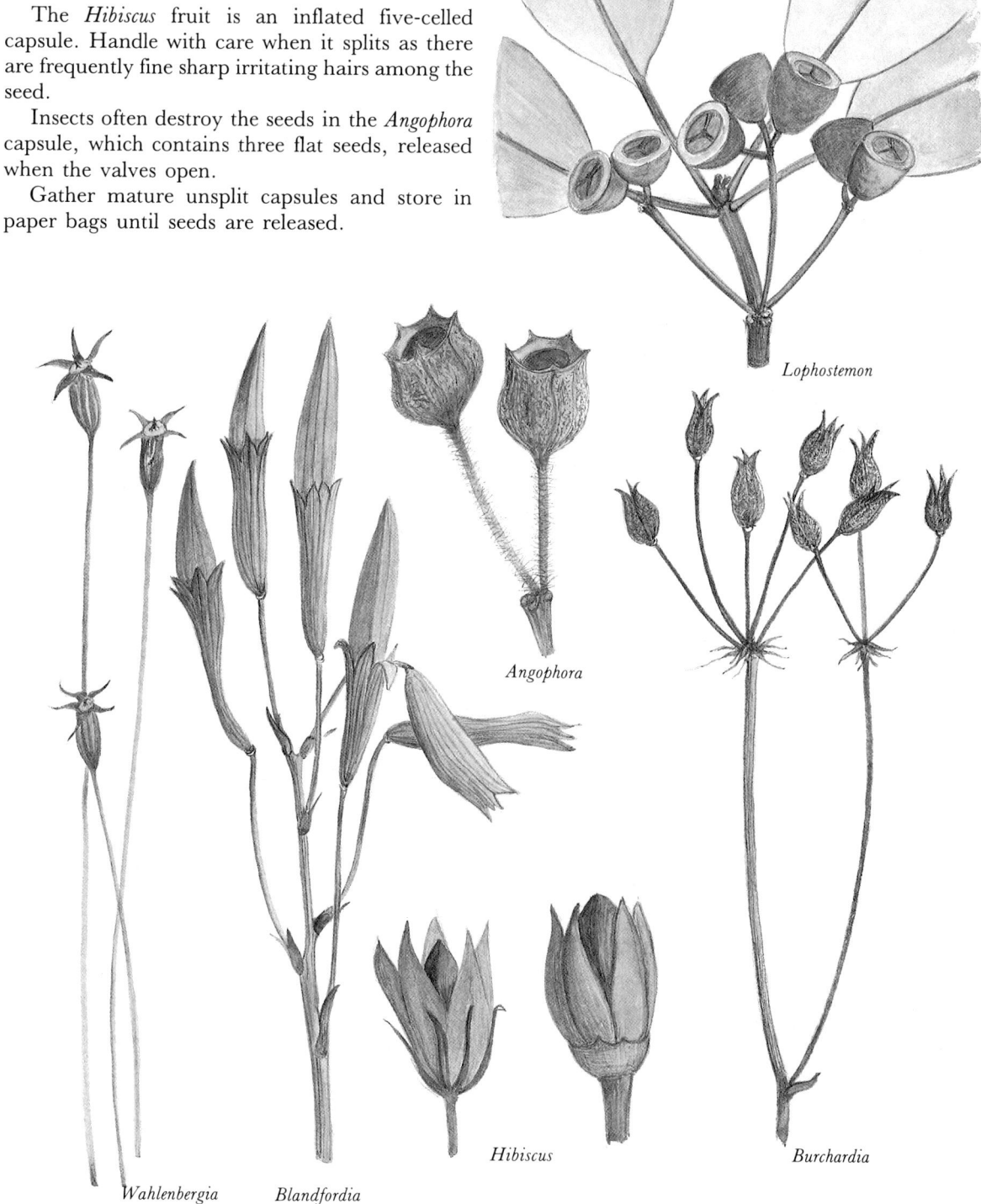

Capsules

The fruit of eucalypts vary greatly in shape and size. Usually seed is retained for only a limited period before the valves open. Mature fruit can be collected at any time and kept in a paper bag until the valves open. Most capsules also contain unfertilised ovules, resembling fine brown chaff, which can be stored with the seed.

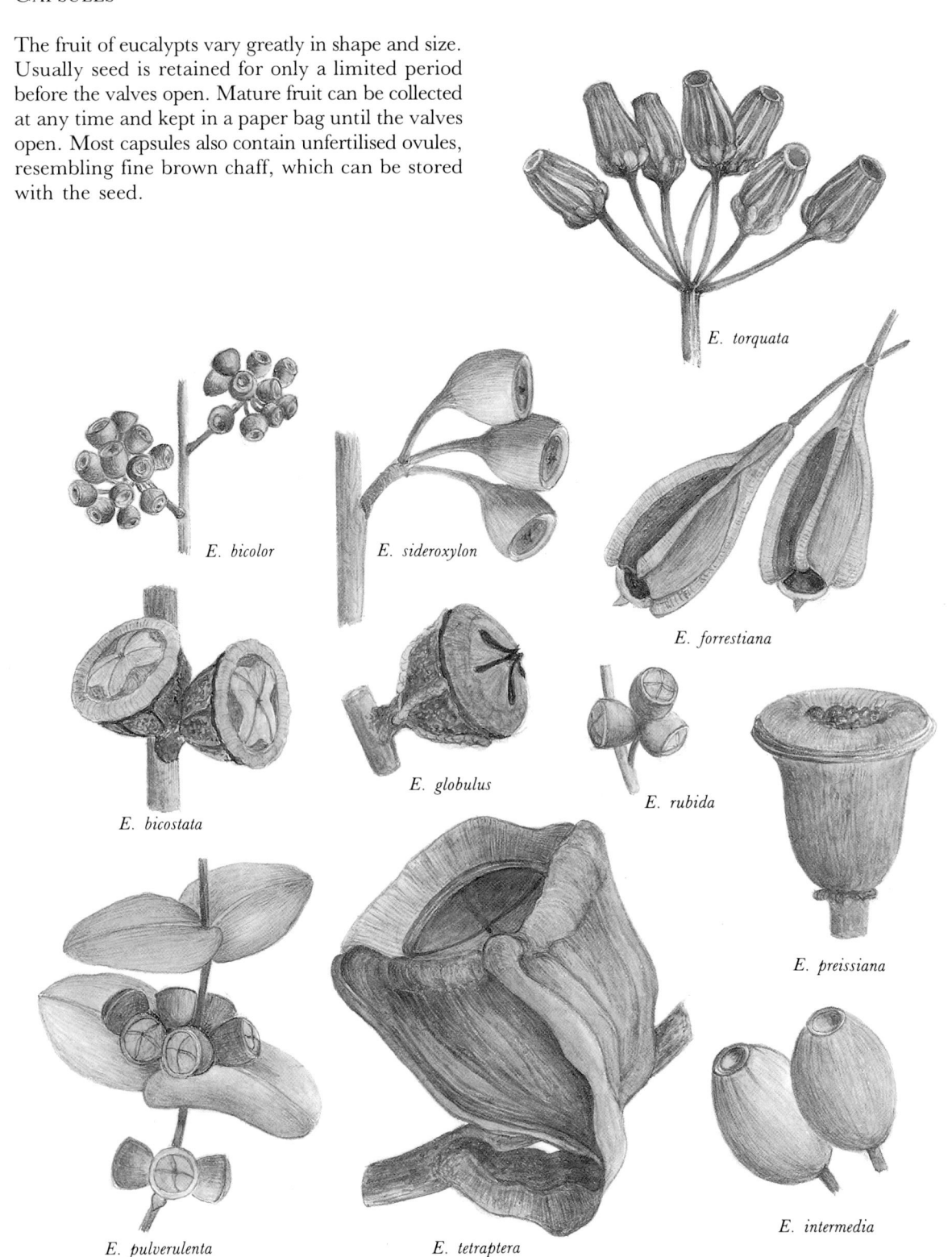

E. torquata

E. bicolor

E. sideroxylon

E. forrestiana

E. bicostata

E. globulus

E. rubida

E. preissiana

E. pulverulenta

E. tetraptera

E. intermedia

FRUIT AND SEED COLLECTING

Capsules

When seed is to be gathered from tall trees, commercial seed merchants spread sheets over the ground to collect it as it is dispersed.

For small quantities of seed, throw a fishing line with a lead sinker attached over a branch and pull it down gently to obtain the fruit.

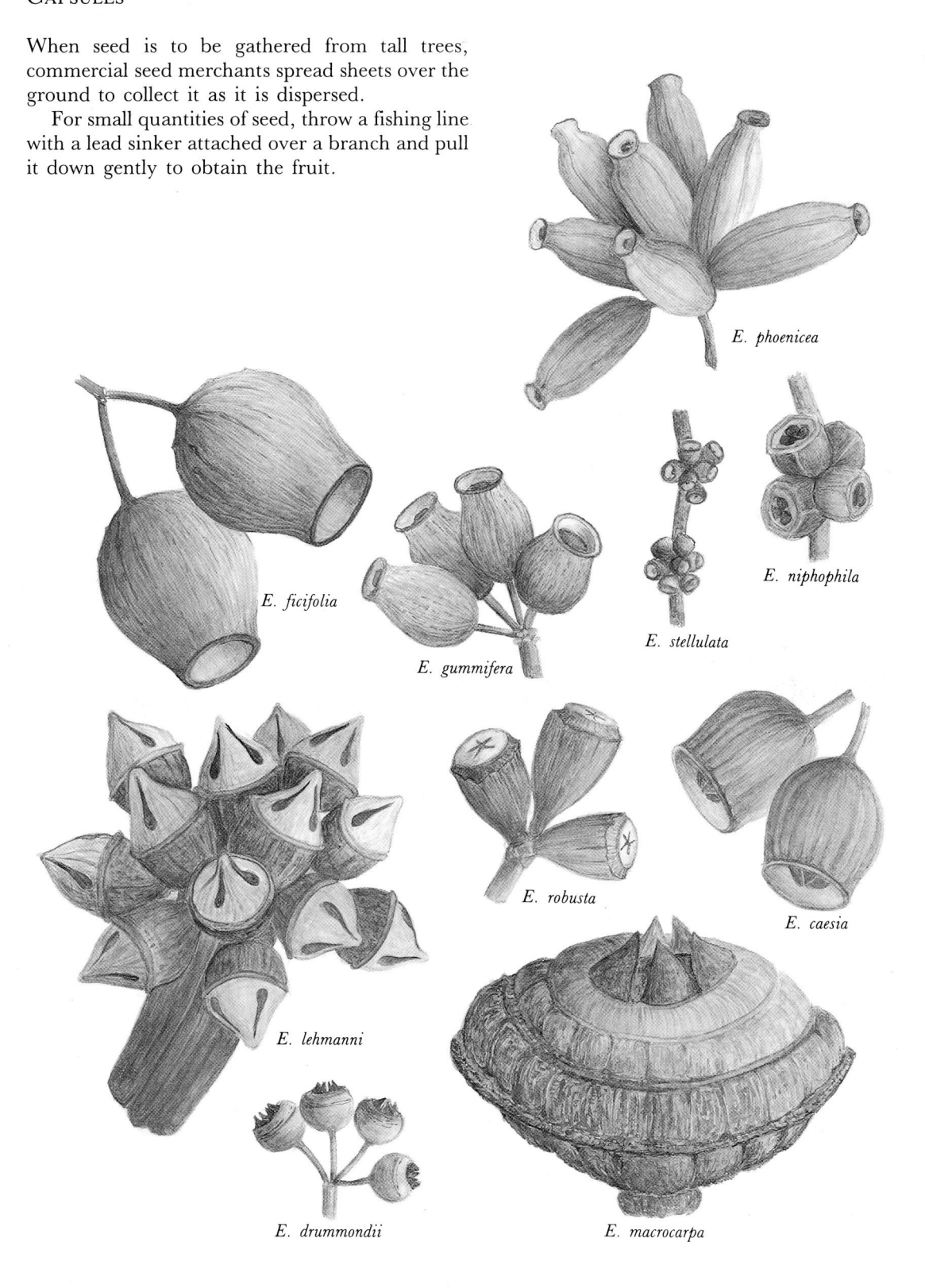

E. phoenicea

E. ficifolia

E. gummifera

E. stellulata

E. niphophila

E. robusta

E. caesia

E. lehmanni

E. drummondii

E. macrocarpa

Capsules

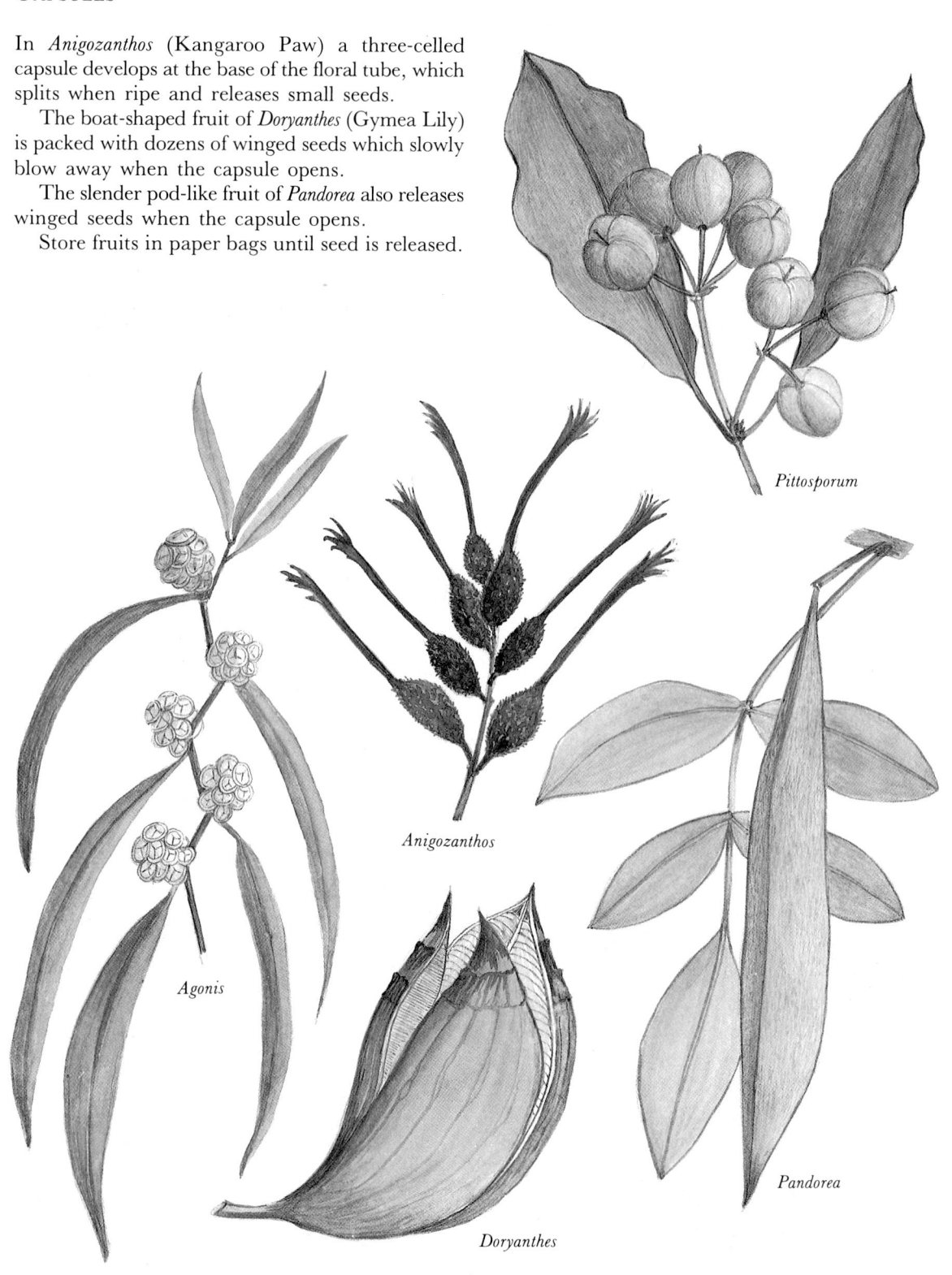

In *Anigozanthos* (Kangaroo Paw) a three-celled capsule develops at the base of the floral tube, which splits when ripe and releases small seeds.

The boat-shaped fruit of *Doryanthes* (Gymea Lily) is packed with dozens of winged seeds which slowly blow away when the capsule opens.

The slender pod-like fruit of *Pandorea* also releases winged seeds when the capsule opens.

Store fruits in paper bags until seed is released.

Pittosporum

Agonis

Anigozanthos

Doryanthes

Pandorea

DRUPES AND FLESHY FRUIT

Drupes generally fall to the ground where they can be easily collected. Numbers of drupes are produced on the pendulous spikes of palms and fall when ripe. Collect only freshly fallen fruit.

Persoonia drupes will fall when ripe. The outer fleshy covering should be removed by sealing the drupes in a plastic bag with a small amount of water and leaving them to ferment in the sun. After a week or two the rotted material can be rinsed away and the seed cases well washed and dried.

The seed of soft fleshy fruit such as *Acmena* and *Syzygium* can be easily removed and dried before storing.

Acmena

Helicia

Persoonia

Elaeocarpus

FOLLICLES

Although follicles may develop slowly, when ripe many open and disperse the seed rapidly, e.g. *Lomatia*. Woody *Hakea* follicles vary in size (small to quite large) and remain unopened on the plant for an indefinite period. When the branch dies, usually after fire, the valves open and release two winged seeds. *H. microcarpa* is an exception to this rule—seeds are released when ripe. *Xylomelum* and *Lambertia* take twelve months or more for a few follicles to develop. Older well developed follicles can be collected and stored in paper bags until the fruit dries and splits to release two winged seeds.

Hakea laurina

Hakea microcarpa

Lomatia

Lambertia

Hakea sericea

Hakea pyconeura

Xylomelum

GREVILLEAS

The shapes and sizes of *Grevillea* follicles are many and varied, often striated, sometimes hard and woody, small or very large. They can be green today but the seed gone by tomorrow. When the follicles begin to open, gather well developed fruit and store in a paper bag for a few days. Usually there are two seeds in each follicle, but sometimes only one.

G. laurifolia

G. venusta

G. buxifolia

G. baueri

G. mucronulata

G. juniperina

G. banksii

BRACHYCHITON, TELOPEA, STENOCARPUS, ALLOXYLON, HOYA

The fruit of *Brachychiton* is a hard tough woody follicle which splits when ripe and slowly releases many yellowish seeds, which should be handled with care as they are surrounded by numerous sharp hairs.

The fruit in the genera *Telopea, Stenocarpus* and *Alloxylon* are follicles which split when ripe, revealing two rows of winged seeds. Seeds can be removed or well developed follicles sealed in a paper bag until the seeds are released.

The fruit of *Hoya* is also a follicle. Only a few fruit develop from each flowering head. When ripe the fruit splits along one side, sometimes unexpectedly, releasing a mass of seeds with long, silky white hairs.

Stenocarpus

Brachychiton

Hoya

Telopea

Alloxylon

BANKSIAS

Although there are large numbers of flowers in a Banksia head, few fruit develop; frequently only a cone of spent flowers remains.

Fertilised Banksia flowers form follicles which may take twelve months to mature. Most Banksias retain their mature seeds in closed follicles but some species, e.g. *Banksia integrifolia*, shed their seed when ripe. Others like *B. cunninghamii* open and release their seed over a period.

Seeds from closed follicles will be released when the branch dies, often after a bushfire. Heat treatment is required to obtain seeds from collected material. Cones placed in a hot oven will open quickly, but cones left in a warm oven, cooling overnight, will open without risk of damage to the seed. Alternatively, the cones may be passed quickly over an open fire. Pairs of winged seeds separated by a woody plate can be knocked from the cone by tapping it on a hard surface.

Mature fruit may be collected at any time.

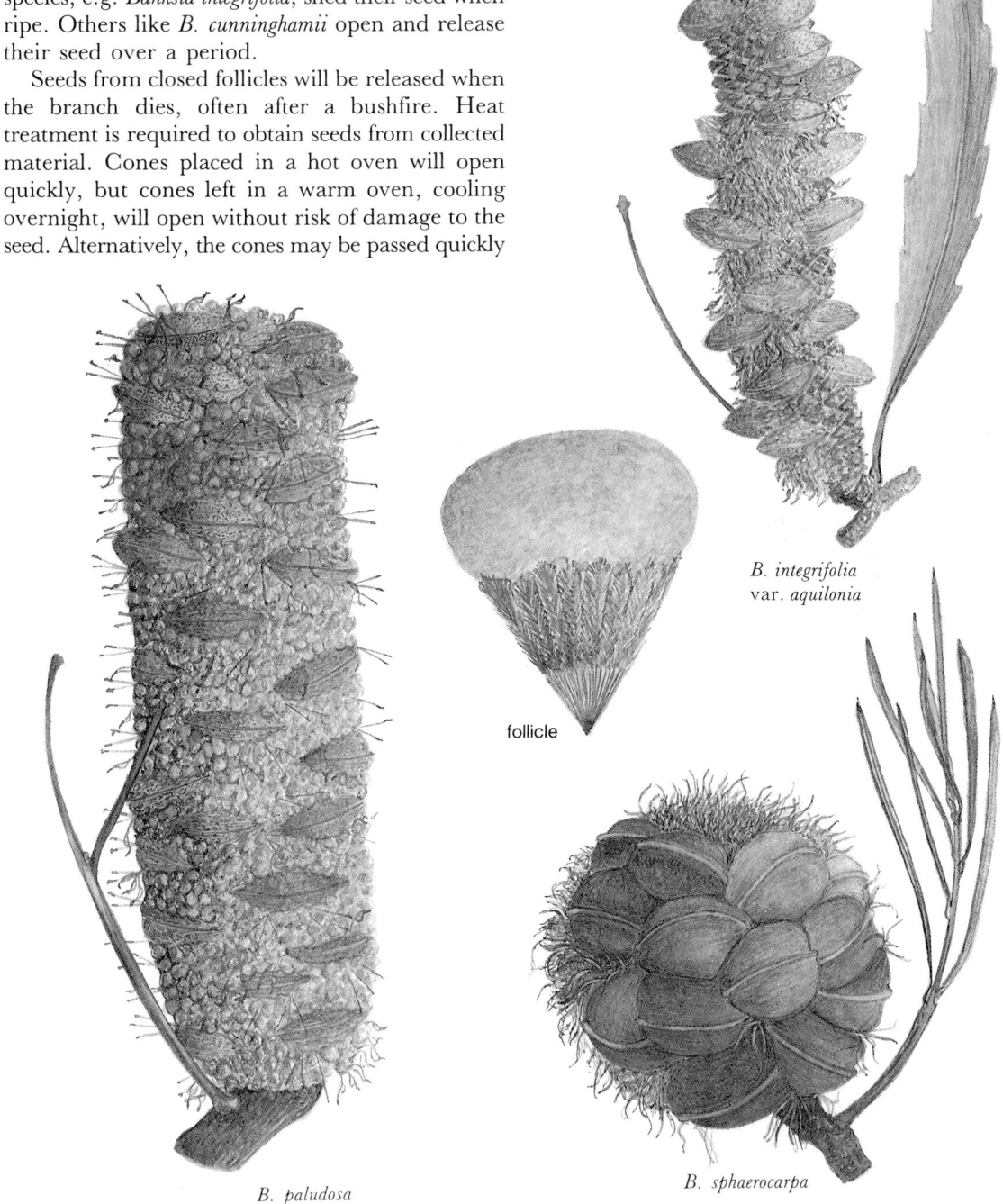

B. integrifolia var. *aquilonia*

follicle

B. paludosa

B. sphaerocarpa

LEGUMES OR PODS

There are many different pea flowers with fruit of various shapes which follow a similar pattern of releasing their seed while the pod is still attached to the plant. In some species pods open only slightly to release the seed slowly, while on hot days pods of some other species will burst open explosively, distributing seed over a wide area, e.g. *Hovea*.

When seed is ripening collect pods and allow to dehisce in a paper bag.

Large-fruiting types, e.g. *Castanospermum* and *Milletia*, often drop the complete fruit, and the pod opens on the ground. Both species have very thin testa, and should be sown soon after collection.

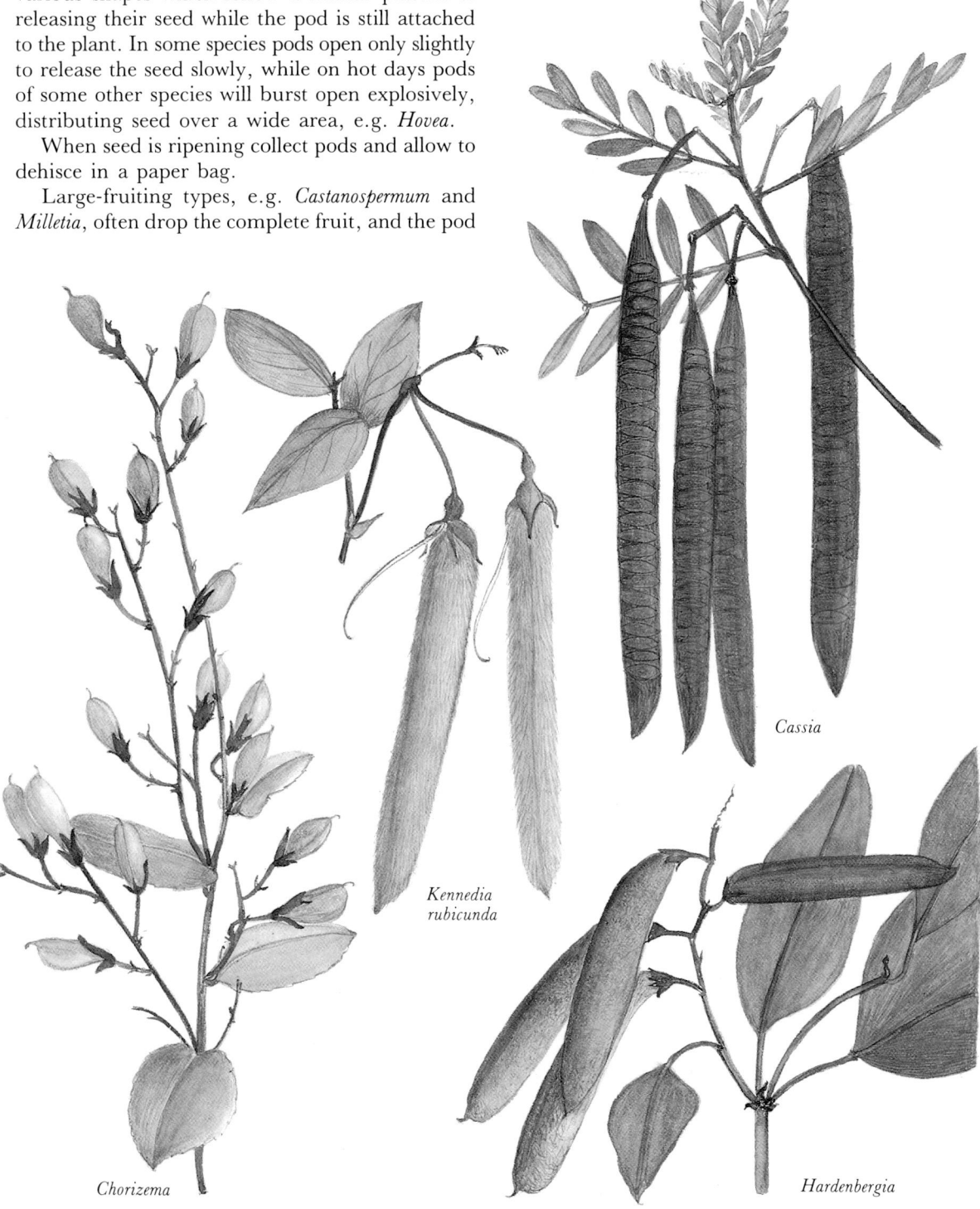

Cassia

Kennedia rubicunda

Chorizema

Hardenbergia

FRUIT AND SEED COLLECTING 49

Pod-bearing Plants

Aotus	*Gastrolobium*	*Mirbelia*
Barklya	*Glycine*	*Phyllota*
Bossiaea	*Gompholobium*	*Platylobium*
Brachysema	*Goodia*	*Pultenaea*
Castanospermum	*Hardenbergia*	*Templetonia*
Chorizema	*Hovea*	*Swainsona*
Crotalaria	*Indigofera*	(includes
Daviesia	*Jacksonia*	*Clianthus*)
Dillwynia	*Kennedia*	

Kennedia coccinea

Gompholobium

Pultenaea

Oxylobium

Dillwynia

Hovea

Acacias

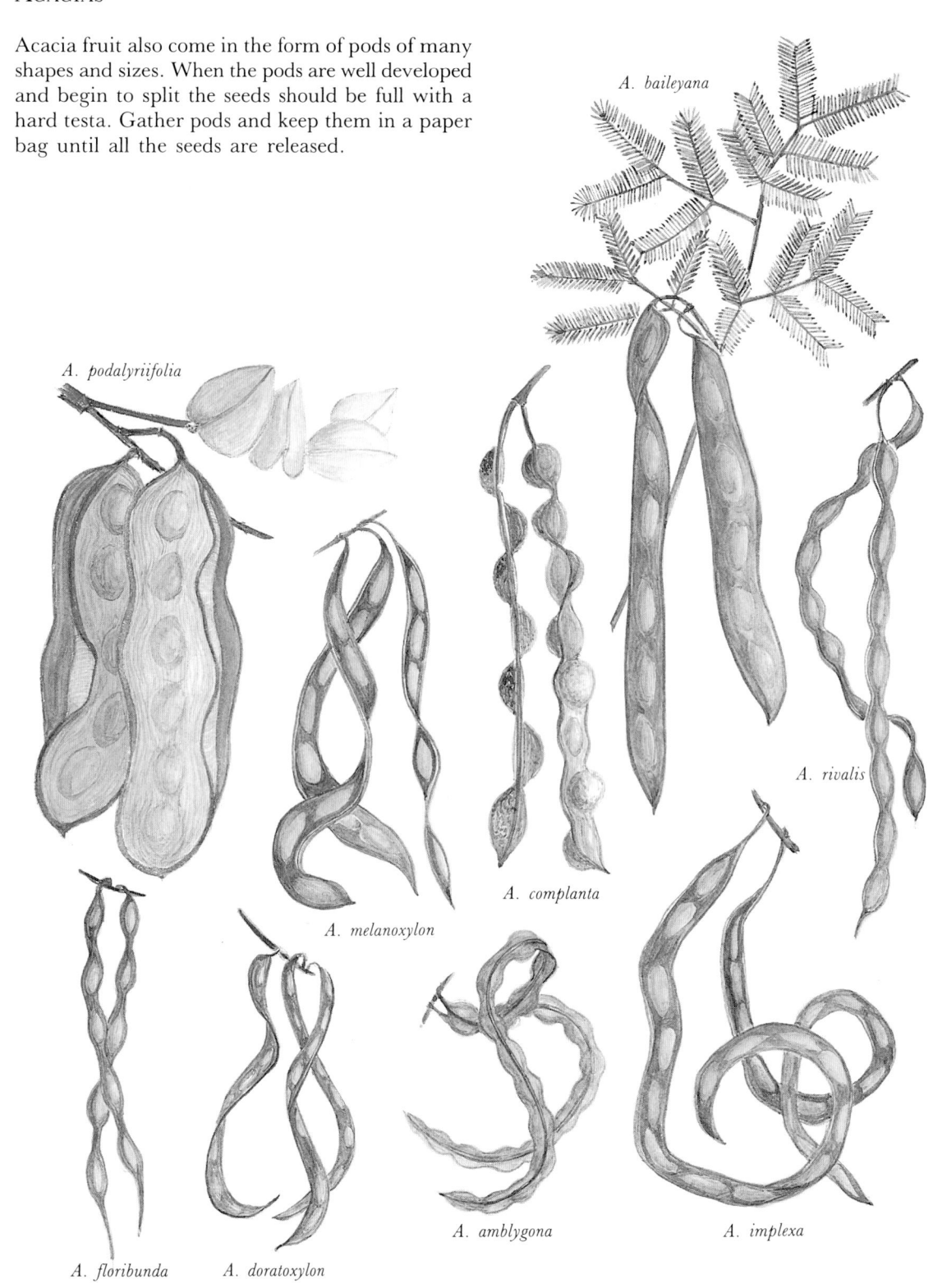

Acacia fruit also come in the form of pods of many shapes and sizes. When the pods are well developed and begin to split the seeds should be full with a hard testa. Gather pods and keep them in a paper bag until all the seeds are released.

A. baileyana

A. podalyriifolia

A. rivalis

A. melanoxylon

A. complanta

A. floribunda

A. doratoxylon

A. amblygona

A. implexa

FRUIT AND SEED COLLECTING 51

NUTS

Small nuts, e.g. *Backhousia*, enclosed in the old flower calyx should be collected when the calyx turns brown. As in *Ceratopetalum* the calyx surrounding the nut changes colour and enlarges, giving a flower-like appearance. Collect mature fruit and store, if necessary, for only a short period.

In *Isopogon* and most *Petrophile* the seed is held by bracts and is released when the branch dies, usually after a bushfire. In some other *Petrophile* the bracts open and release the seed when ripe.

Collect the older well developed fruiting cones with closed bracts and keep them in a warm dry position until the small nuts with tufts of silky hairs are released.

Macadamia, because of the hard woody case surrounding the seed, is often wrongly termed a nut. It is a true follicle.

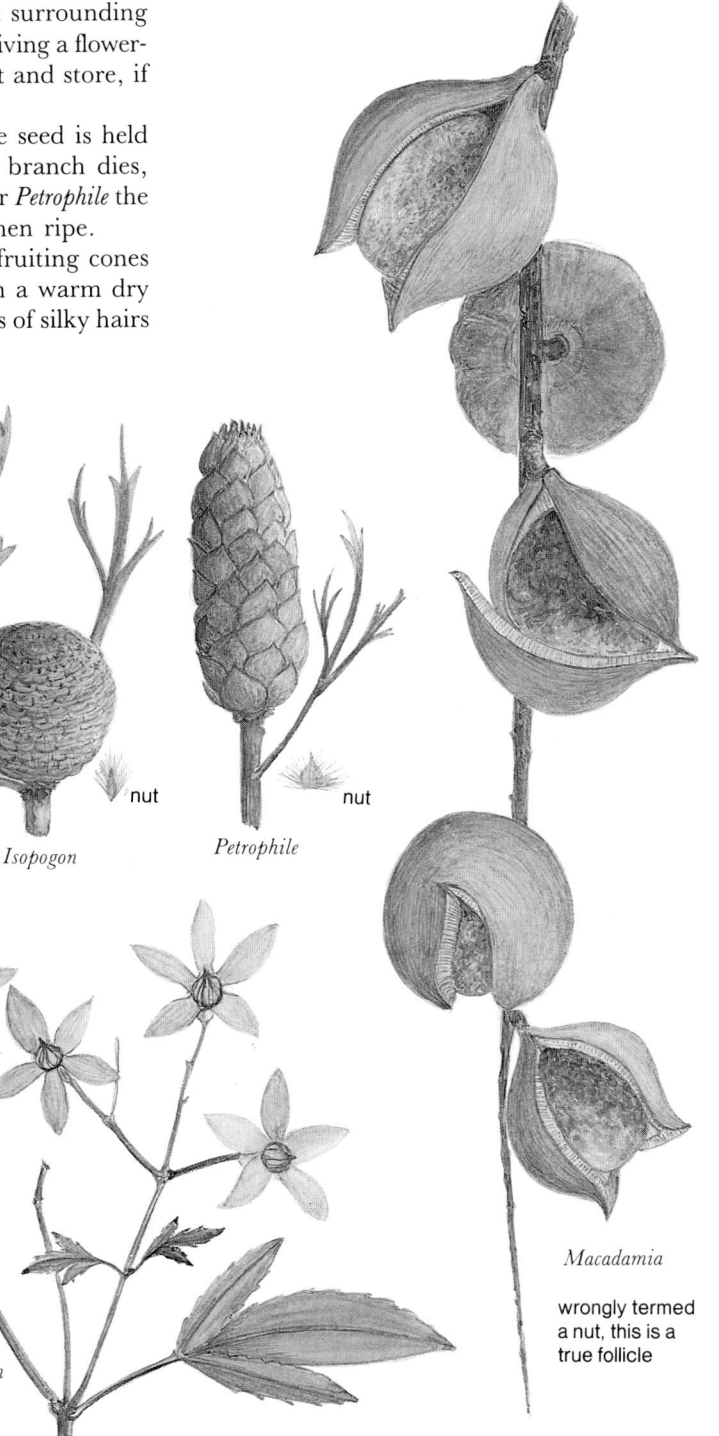

Symphionema

Isopogon nut

Petrophile nut

Ceratopetalum nut

Macadamia

wrongly termed a nut, this is a true follicle

SCHIZOCARPS

The fruit of both *Prostanthera* and *Westringia* are schizocarps. When the floral tube falls from the flower the fruit develops within the calyx. When ripe the fruit divides into four separate carpels each containing a small nut-like seed.

As the calyx changes colour, collect those which feel enlarged.

The fruit of *Geranium* is slender and beak-like with the old calyx at the base. When ripe it splits open from the base and extends upwards into four mericarps which do not release the seed. Collect well developed seed or store fruit in paper bags until the seed is released.

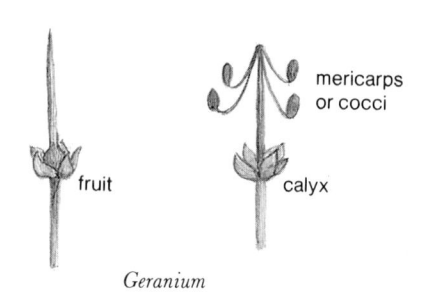

Westringia

Prostanthera

Geranium — fruit, mericarps or cocci, calyx

SEED STORAGE

Always ensure that seed is perfectly dry after it is released from the fruit.

A drying cabinet is ideal when dealing with large quantities of seed, but paper bags hung in airy conditions are sufficient for most growers.

Remove the seed from the fruit if necessary, sometimes cracking open tough hard seed cases.

Make sure no insects or their larvae are present; a dusting of insecticidal powder should give clean seed.

Store seeds in paper envelopes or screw-top jars, labelled with the seed name, place and date of collection.

Fleshy seeds, e.g. *Crinum*, *Calostemma* and *Castanospermum*, should be stored in an open position with free air circulation. (Even then germination may occur.)

Rainforest plants are generally fleshy drupes and lose their viability rapidly, so they are best sown soon after collection. If necessary they can be stored temporarily in a sealed plastic bag kept in the refrigerator.

SEED CHARACTERISTICS

Like fruits, seeds are diverse in shape and size.

In achenes and cypselas the seed is enclosed in a thin case which readily permits water to penetrate and reach the seed.

The seeds of berries are often angular and small, packed neatly in a fleshy surround.

The seed of capsules vary from fine dust-like seed as in *Wahlenbergia* to small to medium in *Eucalyptus*, slender in *Callistemon*, fleshy in *Crinum*, winged in *Pandorea* and sticky in *Pittosporum*.

Drupes and fleshy fruit have a woody case of various thicknesses surrounding the seed. In *Persoonia* the woody case is extremely hard and waterproof, leading to difficulties in germinating the seed, while the drupaceous fruit of *Syzygium* and *Acmena* have a thin case surrounding the seed which allows water to penetrate readily.

Cycads and palms have a tough woody case which slowly permits water to enter the seed.

The seed of follicles, particularly in the Proteaceae family, are frequently winged, e.g. *Banksia*. Sometimes the seed of *Grevillea* may have a small wing. In *Brachychiton* the seeds are nut-like.

The seed may be enclosed in a woody case which may be quite large, e.g. *Macadamia*. The woody case splits readily when subjected to moisture. In contrast, the fruit of *Conospermum* is small and cone-shaped and does not readily split to allow water to enter the seed. *Isopogon* and *Petrophile* have a thin case which breaks down slowly. The fruit of some nuts are small, surrounded by a persistent calyx, as in *Ceratopetalum*. In *Verticordia* the nut is also surrounded by a persistent calyx and large numbers of the fruit produced are infertile.

Pea and legume seed vary from large, with a thin testa, e.g. *Castanospermum*, to medium sized seeds with a tough testa that repels water, e.g. *Acacia*.

Many seeds of legumes are kidney-shaped, e.g. *Hardenbergia*, and have a white fleshy ring (an aril, caruncle or strophile) around the stalk or funicle which connects the seed to the ovary. The aril is conspicuous when the seed is fresh; as it dries out, turns brown and falls off, it leaves a scar known as a hilum. At one side of the hilum is a small opening, the micropyle, through which the radicle or developing root emerges during germination.

Schizocarp fruit divide into separate mesocarps or cocci each of which contain a seed in the case or carpel, e.g. *Geranium*.

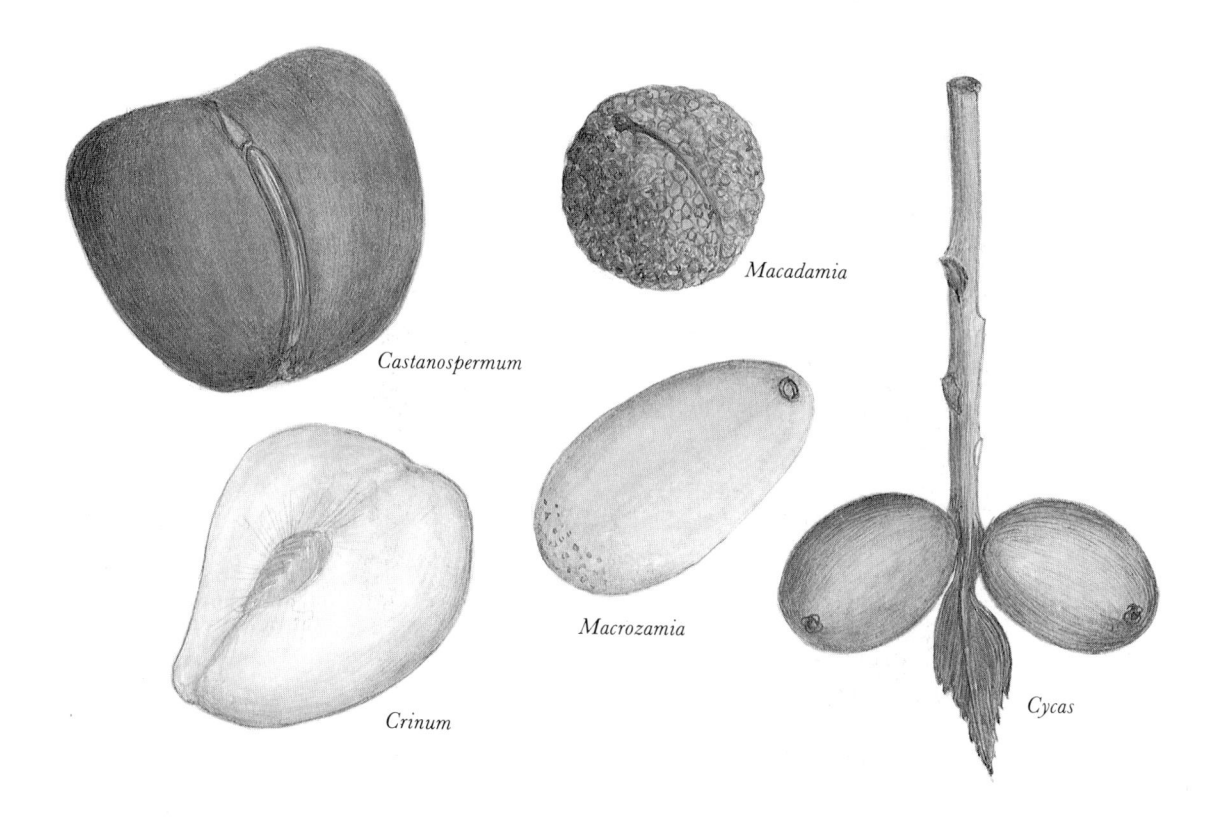

Castanospermum

Macadamia

Crinum

Macrozamia

Cycas

Banksia seeds

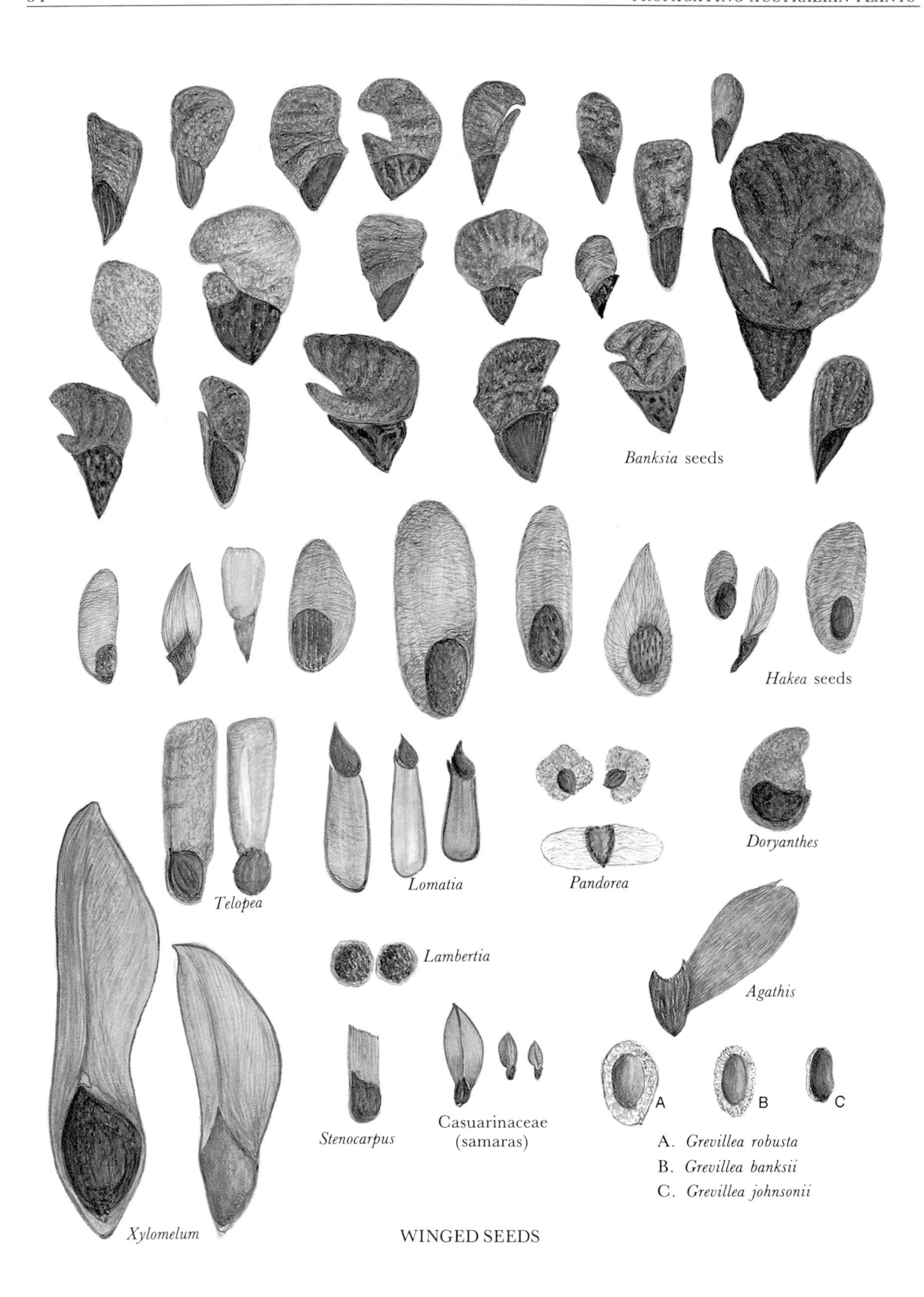

Hakea seeds

Telopea

Lomatia

Pandorea

Doryanthes

Lambertia

Agathis

Stenocarpus

Casuarinaceae
(samaras)

A. *Grevillea robusta*
B. *Grevillea banksii*
C. *Grevillea johnsonii*

Xylomelum

WINGED SEEDS

FRUIT AND SEED COLLECTING

Acacia seed with funicles

Paraserianthes *Cassia* *Lysiphyllum* *Kennedia*

Grevillea seed

Isopogon *Petrophile*

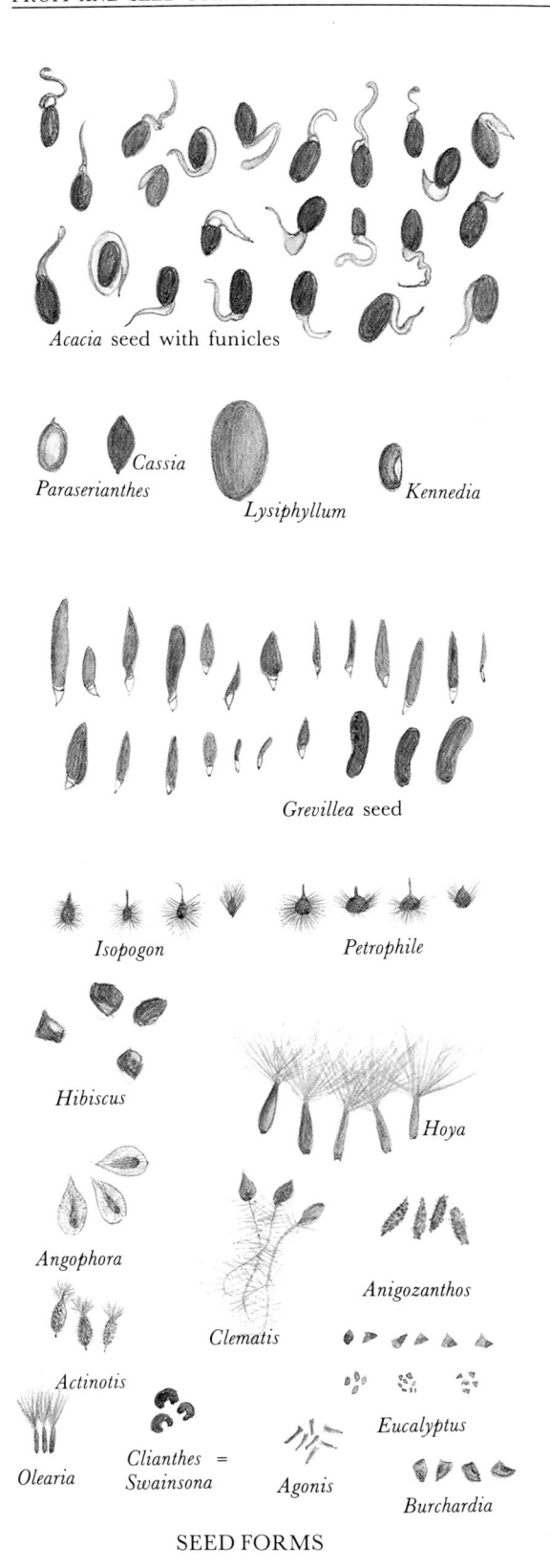

Hibiscus

Hoya

Angophora

Anigozanthos

Clematis

Actinotis

Olearia *Clianthes = Swainsona* *Agonis* *Eucalyptus* *Burchardia*

SEED FORMS

VIABILITY

Raising seed allows plants to be brought into cultivation by enabling the production of large numbers of seedlings, important in the development of plant breeding, in producing new hybrid species and for purposes of reafforestation, e.g. *Eucalyptus*. Although most plants produce viable seed, some plants produce only a few seeds which will germinate, e.g. *Conospermum*.

Many seeds presenting a normal appearance will contain an undeveloped embryo. Potentially viable embryos can be damaged by insect attack and be unable to germinate.

Seeds of some species contain substances which inhibit their germination until the substances are leached away.

Some seed, particularly those from areas of snow and freezing conditions, have a dormancy period which must be broken before germination.

In other species, although a few seeds may germinate spasmodically in nature, they generally require the action of fire or the association of different factors such as concentration of substances, e.g. potassium, or the stimulation of mycorrhiza spores to bring about germination.

Seed of some species, e.g. *Persoonia*, is enclosed in a woody case which does not open or split readily when ripe. This prevents water from entering and reaching the embryo to bring about germination. In the genus *Persoonia* germination may be erratic even if water does reach the embryo. This is not fully understood but it may be due to a dormancy period which is hard to break.

The testa of some seeds, e.g. *Acacia*, is tough and covered with a waxy outer coating which repels water. In nature this covering may be weakened by sand, ants or fire action after falling from the plant. To activate germination in cultivation such seeds must be treated by sandpapering and soaking in boiling water to allow water to reach the embryo.

Fine seed, e.g. *Melaleuca*, generally germinates freely.

PREPARATION OF SEED FOR SOWING

Hard Testa Seed

Hard testa seed cases repel water, preventing its penetration to the embryo. To make germination more certain, such seed cases must be weakened. They can be treated with strong acids such as sulphuric acid, but care must be taken when handling dangerous substances of this sort.

An easier way of removing the outer waxy coating is to rub the seeds lightly between two pieces of diamond-grit sandpaper, or use a sanding block covered with sandpaper. Be careful not to destroy the seed by exerting too much pressure when rubbing. After sanding, place seeds in a small container and pour boiling water over them. Leave to soak for several hours or overnight. Fertile seeds will swell. Discard any seeds which float.

Use this sandpapering and boiling water treatment for obstinate seeds such as some species of *Grevillea*.

Seed requiring sandpaper and boiling water treatment:

Acacia	*Crotalaria*	*Kennedia*
Aotus	*Daviesia*	*Mirbelia*
Barklya	*Dillwynia*	*Phyllota*
Bossiaea	*Glycine*	*Platylobium*
Brachysema	*Gompholobium*	*Pultenaea*
Cassia	*Hardenbergia*	*Sphaerolobium*
(now *Senna*)	*Hovea*	*Swainsona*
Chorizema	*Indigofera*	*Templetonia*
Clianthus (now included with *Swainsona*)	*Jacksonia*	*Viminaria*

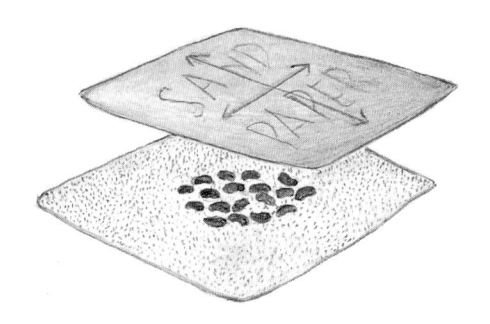

Seeds with Dormancy Periods

Some seeds have a dormancy period which must be broken before the seed will germinate, requiring use of a method known as stratification.

Secure the seeds in a plastic bag with a mixture of wet sand and peat and hold in a refrigerator at 2°C for at least six weeks. The seeds can then be sown in a seed box. If germination does not occur within a reasonable time, say 30 days, the seed can be stratified for another three weeks.

Stratification can also be tried with seeds which have no dormancy period but are difficult to germinate.

Seeds needing stratification treatment
Aciphylla
Celmissia sp.
Eucalyptus niphophylla
Eucalyptus pauciflora
Pimelea
Ranunculus (Alpine species)
Richea

Difficult Seeds

Many plants regarded as difficult to germinate produce large numbers of infertile seeds. This is common in *Verticordia*. Other plants produce large numbers of apparently fertile seeds of which few, if any, germinate. In the field *Persoonia pinifolia*, for example, normally produces few if any seedlings, but on rare occasions there is a prolific germination.

Seeds from such plants sown in seed beds over a number of years generally follow the same pattern of sporadic germination.

Seeds difficult to germinate

Astroloma	*Micromyrtus*
Brachyloma	*Persoonia*
Conospermum	*Styphelia*
Darwinia	*Thryptomene*
Leucopogon	*Verticordia*
Lissanthe	

Rutaceae

Most seed of the Rutaceae family, in particular the eastern coast species, are difficult to germinate. Numerous seeds are produced, which fall to the ground when ripe. Over the years sporadic germination may occur, but only after a bushfire do large numbers of seedlings appear. Mycorrhiza in the soil, stimulated by the heat, assist in bringing about germination after the fire has broken the testa of the seed.

These conditions can be reproduced by sowing seed in soil gathered from an area where the plants grow naturally, covering the seed box with small twigs and dry leaves to a depth of 2-3 cm and setting fire to the litter, raising the temperature of the soil surface to 93°C.

Seeds treated by fire

Asterolasia	*Eriostemon*
Boronia	*Phebalium*
Correa	*Philotheca*
Crowea	*Zieria*

Fleshy Fruit

Fruits which have a fleshy layer on the surface, e.g. cycads and palms, contain substances which inhibit the germination of seed.

The fleshy outer covering should be removed before sowing. Large numbers of seeds can be sealed in a plastic bag with a small amount of water and left to ferment in the sun. Then wash or leach the seed for about three weeks by placing it in a nylon stocking hung in a toilet cistern. This speeds up the germination process.

Alternatively the seed can be sown after the fleshy layer has been removed and the inhibiting subtances removed by continual watering; using this method the seed may take several months to germinate.

Leaching by the cistern method often helps to bring about germination in *Eriostemon* and *Boronia*.

Seeds requiring leaching

Boronia	*Eriostemon*
Cordyline	*Palms*
Davidsonia	*Passiflora*
Endriandra	*Pittosporum*

6 Germinating Seeds

Seeds require moisture, air and warmth for successful germination. Some seeds will germinate in a few days, others take up to twelve months, but the average is about three or four weeks.

Using sterilised soil, watering during the cooler part of the day, and treating the soil with a fungicide, e.g. Fongarid or Terrazol, will help control fungal diseases. Damping off is a fungal disease (common in *Telopea*) which causes the complete collapse and loss of seedlings.

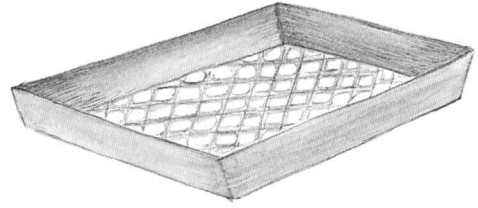

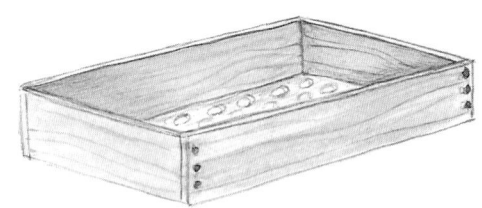

SOIL

Soil should be friable allowing free air circulation and free drainage. For general use, 8 parts of quartz river sand with 1 part peat moss is satisfactory. Vermiculite or perlite may be used instead of sand.

Sterilise the soil by heating at 60°C for thirty minutes and wet it thoroughly before sowing seeds.

SEED BOXES

Seed beds are used for propagating seedlings in large numbers, but for small quantities seed boxes are more convenient and easily handled.

Seed boxes may be commercial plastic planter trays, wooden boxes with drainage holes, plastic punnets or pots. The ideal depth for smaller seeds, giving good drainage, is 75 mm. Trays to a depth of 150 mm can be used for larger seeds, e.g. *Castanospermum*, cycads and *Macadamia*. These seeds can also be sown in separate containers.

Level the prepared soil in the seed box with a thin piece of flat wood or similar, water the soil before sowing, and always label the boxes with the name of the seed and the date of sowing.

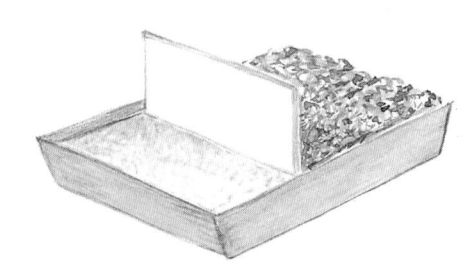

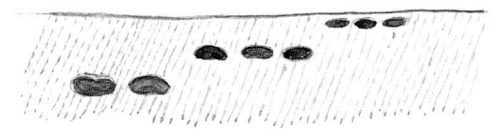

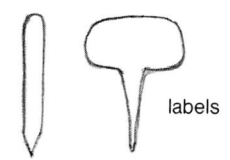

FINE SEED

Sow fine seed such as *Callistemon, Calothamnus, Leptospermum* and *Wahlenbergia* in a seed tray filled almost to the top. To give an even distribution of fine seed over the soil surface, mix the seed with dry sand, then drizzle the mixture slowly over the soil from an envelope or a piece of folded paper. Tap gently for good distribution.

Cover the seed by sprinkling with sand or drizzling it between your hands. Be careful not to cover the seed too deeply. The general rule is to cover the seed with soil to two or three times the seed's thickness. It is important not to sow seed too deeply as its stored energy may be exhausted before the plumule reaches the surface. Water well, using a fine hand spray to prevent seeds being washed out.

The seed box must be kept damp, so keep it in a protected position. Covering the box with a sheet of glass will minimise evaporation. An alternative to surface watering is to stand the box in a shallow tray of water until germination commences.

After seeds germinate surface watering with a fine spray is advised.

MEDIUM-SIZED SEEDS

Sow the seeds of *Acacia* (previously treated by the sandpaper and boiling water method), *Banksia, Hakea, Grevillea* and other medium sized seeds in rows, spread them evenly over the soil surface, or sow them in shallow grooves.

Cover with moist washed granular sand to two or three times the thickness of the seed and water well with a fine spray. To help control damping off, treat initially with a fungicide, e.g. Fongarid, Terrazole or Aliette, using 1/3 of a teaspoon to 5 litres of water. Do not allow the soil to dry out between waterings.

Where only a few seedlings are required the seed can be germinated on paper towelling (or in an egg carton). Fold thoroughly saturated paper and put in a plastic container (ice-cream or margarine containers are ideal), adding a little extra water to ensure against drying out. Place the seeds on the paper and cover the container with the lid. Keep covered for at least a week until a small white root projects from the seed.

The seed can then be moved to a small pot filled with potting soil, make a small hole for the developing root to fit into. Cover the seed with soil to two or three times its thickness and water well. Stand the pot in a well lighted position. In about a week the cotyledons should appear, then the small shoot or plumule develops. Treat the emerging plant in the same way as other seedlings.

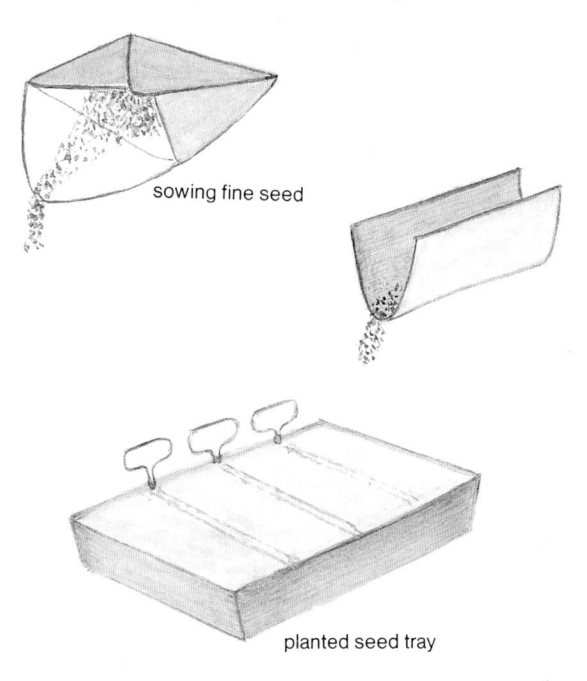

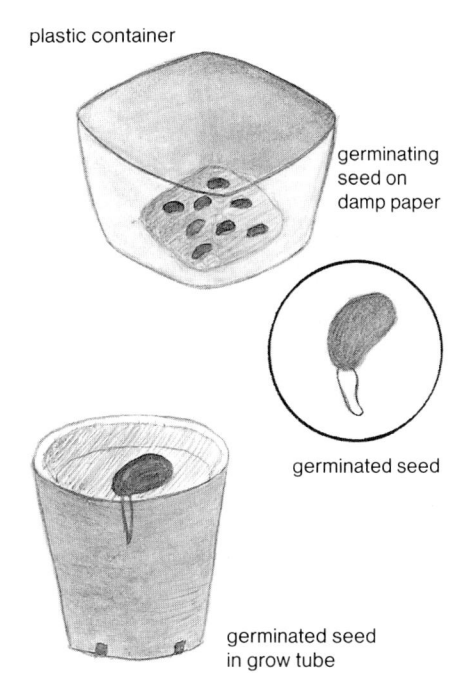

sowing fine seed

planted seed tray

plastic container

germinating seed on damp paper

germinated seed

germinated seed in grow tube

LARGE SEEDS

The large seeds of *Castanospermum, Crinum,* cycads, *Davidsonia, Endriandra, Macadamia* and palms can be germinated in individual containers about 150 mm deep, as the seed makes a deep root before a leaf shoot develops. The seedlings can be grown on in the same container. If a number of large seeds are to be grown in a deep box or pot, special care must be taken when transplanting them.

Press the seed into the potting mix to a depth of half to two-thirds their thickness. Water well, and keep in a protected position.

- **Palm seeds** can be germinated in saturated peat moss sealed in a plastic bag. When roots begin to emerge (which may take six months) the seed can be planted in potting soil and grown on like other seedlings.
- **Cycad seeds** have no dormant period. Once the ovule has been fertilised the embryo begins to grow. By the time the fruit falls to the ground the cotyledons have begun to grow into the endosperm. The embryo continues growing until the radicle, protected by the coleorhiza cap, exerts enough pressure on the seed case to split it around the micropyle, and the root tip, protected by the cap, emerges. This is a slow process, however. From fertilisation to the point where the primary root emerges may take 12 to 18 months or more. The emerging primary root grows quickly downwards into the soil, becoming thick and stout like a carrot.

Soaking the seed in a 2% solution of gibberellic acid for one hour has been shown to speed up germination.

From the primary root, secondary roots develop. Those growing from the upper part form specialised coralloid roots, which grow upwards to the soil surface.

The cotyledons are slowly withdrawn from the seed, leaving only the tips attached, and the first leaf appears between the cotyledons. As growth develops the cotyledons slowly shrivel and ultimately the seed case is shed.

The primary root system develops a deep taproot and further adventitious roots arise. Coralloid roots become more numerous.

The secondary leaf appears one or two months after the first leaf, but the formation of leaves is very slow, only five or six leaves appearing in the first year.

GROWING SEEDLINGS

After seedlings appear, continue daily watering in the cooler part of the day. Treating again with a fungicide is also recommended.

Soil Mixes

Various soil mixes may be used for growing on plants in containers. Whatever mix is used should permit free movement of water through the medium and encourage the development of a strong root system. Small quantities of soil may be mixed using:
  2 parts well rotted leaf mould
  1 part coarse river sand
  1 part hard clinker ash
  ½ part tennis court loam

Plants may be potted into this mix and growth stimulated by the application of a slow release fertiliser on the soil surface or by periodic applications of a liquid fertiliser such as Aquasol.

In commercial nurseries it is the practice to add fertilisers to the soil mix to stimulate growth, with the further use of fertilisers in the watering system or slow release fertilisers on the potted soil surface.

Below are two examples of soil mixes to which fertilisers are added. These may be modified to suit a particular purpose, e.g. mixes using composted pine bark fines or for growing proteaceous plants.

For good results a pH of 6-6.5 should be maintained.

Mix 1 (as used in a large native plant nursery)
  1 part peat moss
  1 part sterilised rice hulls
  1 part perlite
Fertilisers per cubic metre (*Note:* quantities in brackets are for a 10 litre/2 gallon bucket):
  2 kg (20 g) Osmocote Blue (17 parts nitrogen, 1.6 parts phosphorus, 27 parts potassium)
  2 kg (20 g) Multicote (20.8 parts nitrogen, 10.9 parts potassium)
  1 kg (10 g) trace elements (Micromat)
  1 kg (10 g) iron chelates
  2 kg (20 g) dolomite
  100 ml (1 ml) Wetter Soil

Mix 2 (based on the University of California system and developed some time ago at the Sydney Botànic Gardens):

25% finely sifted peat moss
75% washed coarse quartz river sand
Fertilisers per cubic metre (*Note:* quantities in brackets are for a 10 litre/2 gallon bucket):
   57 g (0.57 g) potassium sulphate
   57 g (0.57 g) potassium nitrate
   84 g (0.84 g) Essminel (mixture of trace elements)
   300 g (3 g) dolomite
   900 g (9 g) superphosphate
   900 g (9 g) blood and bone
   925 g (9.25 g) calcium carbonate
The final pH should be between 5–6.5.

For growing Grevilleas and other Proteaceae the superphosphate should be reduced to 300 g (3 g).

Containers

Light plastic containers, which prevent evaporation through the sides, and can be stored easily, are the most satisfactory pots. Check that there are ample drainage holes in the base.

Grow tubes, 75 mm in diameter and 95 mm deep, are best for general nursery use.

A new container made of compressed peat, 75 mm in diameter and 80 mm deep, is available. Seedlings can be grown in these and planted, container and all, into the ground or potted on.

Tree seedlings, which will receive little attention when planted out, should be potted on in 50 mm square tubes, 125 mm deep.

For large individual seeds, plastic containers 75 mm in diameter and 150 mm deep are the most useful.

Transplanting Seedlings

Fill the potting-on containers with the prepared soil. Tap the pots gently on the bench to firm the soil, and add more if necessary. Make a deep hole in the soil and fill it with water, which should drain away quickly.

Individual seedlings can be pricked out of the seed box, using a small fork or knife, and taking care not to damage the young root system.

Plant the seedling in the hole, and fill in the soil to the same level at which it was previously growing. Water well, and add extra soil if necessary.

Keep the newly potted seedlings in a shady protected position at first before moving them into full sunlight. Water daily in the cool of the day.

Water plants which are subject to damp off (e.g. *Telopea*) with a fungicide solution such as Fongarid at six-weekly intervals during warm weather. Use fungicide sparingly as it can become toxic to some plants. Watch for insect and snail attack.

Seedlings need three to four months to develop a good root system and become established before planting out. Check the root system by gently knocking the seedling out of the pot. There should be good root growth before planting out or potting on into a larger container is contemplated.

shrubby type seedling in grow tube

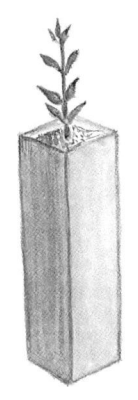

tree seedling in 50 mm square tube

Cordyline sp. seedlings

Seedling Types

It is possible to keep plants growing successfully for long periods in containers. Always pot on into a marginally larger container, e.g. transfer a plant growing in a 100 mm pot to a 125 mm pot.

To transfer a plant into a larger container add sufficient soil in the base to bring the old soil level to the top of the new pot. Fill the outer space with potting soil, water well, and after a few days in a protected position, grow on as before.

Isopogon prostratus

seedling with leaves

seedling with developing phyllodes

Acacia

dicotyledons raised above soil with developing shoot

roots with bacterial nodules

1 *Hovea* 2

Hakea seedling

Carpentaria palm

GERMINATING SEEDS

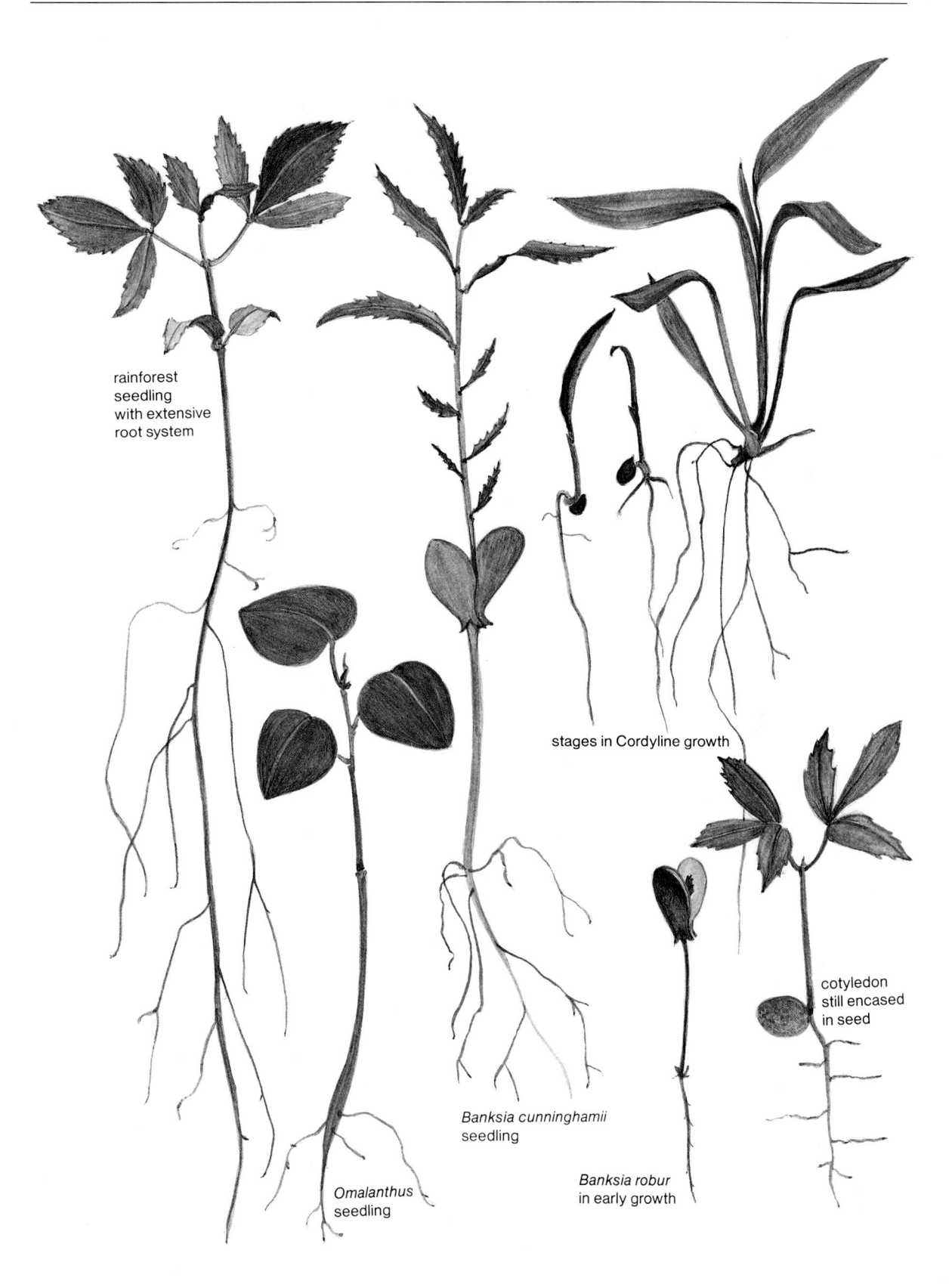

rainforest seedling with extensive root system

stages in Cordyline growth

cotyledon still encased in seed

Omalanthus seedling

Banksia cunninghamii seedling

Banksia robur in early growth

7 Vegetative Propagation

Vegetative propagation, whether from cuttings, layering, division, grafting, budding or tissue culture, enables exact replicas of the parent plant to be reproduced. Seedlings, on the other hand, are individual and may vary from the parent plant. Plants grown from cuttings will often flower within a year, whereas plants grown from seed may take two to five years to reach flowering stage—some species may even take up to ten years to flower. Vegetative propagation is also an advantage where plants are difficult to grow from seed.

Not all plants are suited to vegetative reproduction. Dicotyledonous plants have an outer ring of growth tissue called the cambium layer, within which is the cambium, a ring of cells rich in meristemic tissue. Given suitable conditions this tissue can produce roots from a stem section.

Monocotyledonous plants, with few exceptions, have no cambium layer. They are unable to produce roots on aerial stem sections except where tissue culture is used.

Most dicotyledonous plants can be propagated from plant sections—stems, buds, roots and even leaves in some species. However, some groups, e.g. *Eucalyptus*, appear to contain inhibiting substances which make vegetative propagation from cuttings difficult.

Meristem propagation (see page 16) allows the production of unlimited numbers of plants from the meristemic cells, but this process requires specialist knowledge and expensive equipment.

New Plant Growth

Herbaceous plants, e.g. daisies, which have soft stems, develop new growth which stiffens as it extends. Woody plants develop new growth from terminal and lateral buds which at first grows fairly rapidly and is soft and fleshy. Growth slows down as the plant deposits woody cellulose-strengthening tissues. Carbohydrates are also deposited in the stem tissue which the plant uses as a reserve source of energy.

Cuttings rely on this stored carbohydrate when they are removed from the flow of plant nutrients. Leaves left on the cutting form new tissues by photosynthesis, which enables roots and new growth to develop.

CUTTINGS

Taking cuttings is probably the most commonly used method of vegetative reproduction.

To take cuttings from herbaceous plants select new upper growth which has become firm.

For woody type plants take cuttings of new growth which has become hardened but not woody in texture. To test the maturity of the growth for the cutting, hold the stem and bend the upper part—good cutting material will spring back readily.

Side (lateral) growth appear to give better results than cuttings taken from the top, possibly because of carbohydrate storage in the stems.

Good times to collect cuttings are generally just as the plants are beginning to grow in spring, immediately after flowering or when buds which are swelling in the leaf axils are ready to grow. Firmed new growth, taken in autumn when the stem has a quantity of stored carbohydrates, is also ideal. Experiment by taking cuttings at different times of the year.

Exceptions to these rules are members of the Myrtaceae family. Soft cuttings of Geraldton Wax root more readily if taken in late November but cuttings of *Melaleuca* and *Callistemon* are best taken just after the new growth begins to harden.

Hard woody stems (with the exception of deciduous exotic species) are unsatisfactory for cutting material.

selection of 3 cuttings

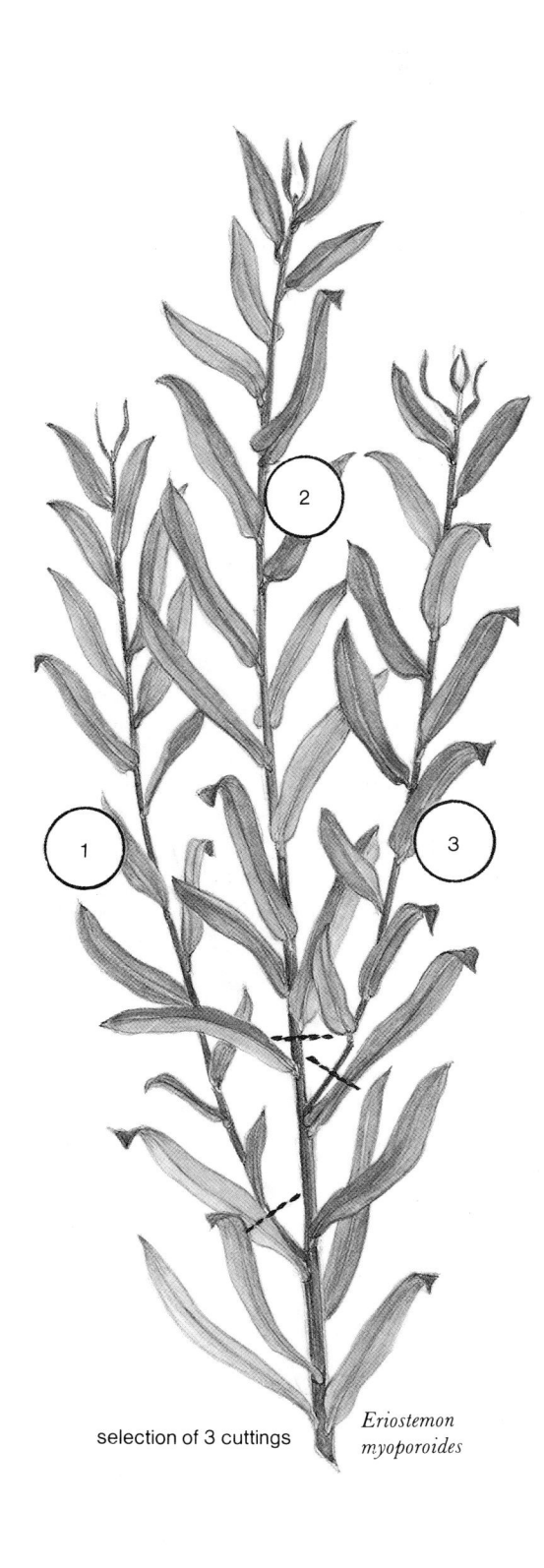

Eriostemon myoporoides

Collecting Cuttings

When collecting cutting material you can maximise your chances of success by taking cuttings from several different plants.

Transpiration through the leaves continues even when the cutting has been removed from the parent plant. As moisture is drawn from the stem, air is drawn in after it and an airlock forms in the lower stem. This can prevent further moisture moving up the stem. To counteract this, take the cutting longer than required (so that the airlocked section can later be trimmed off) and place immediately in a container of water to which a few drops of hormone solution have been added. Formula 20, Hormone 20 or Plant Hormone are all suitable. Alternatively, place cuttings in a moistened plastic bag with plenty of free space, blow up the bag, tie off and keep cool. This method allows cuttings to be transported over a distance, minimising bruising of leaves and stems which could lead to fungal attacks. The bag can be stored briefly in a refrigerator if the cuttings won't be used immediately.

If cuttings are to be posted, wrap them loosely in moist newspaper enclosed in a plastic bag. On their arrival the cuttings should be stood for about an hour in water with a few drops of plant hormone added before preparing them for planting. See page 66.

Sections of the underground stem of monocotyledonous plants such as *Dianella* can be treated in the same manner as stem cuttings.

Leaf Cuttings

Boea hygromatica can be propagated by leaf cuttings. Take the whole leaf with a short leaf stalk, cut the mid-vein underneath the leaf, dust each cut surface with a hormone cutting powder (or dip into a liquid hormone) before placing the leaf on a cutting medium. Firm down and water well.

Root Cuttings

Sections of main roots taken from plants such as *Boronia pinnata* are treated with a cutting hormone and placed vertically in a cutting medium.

How Cuttings Grow

Cuttings should be taken about 10–15 cm long, with as many leaves as possible. The moisture from the cutting medium absorbed by the stem supports the leaves which allow photosynthesis to take place so that new plant tissue and roots can be formed. Any bruised or damaged material should be discarded, as it is liable to fungal attack.

Roots can develop from any part of the cutting in contact with the cutting medium (often from a leaf node). Occasionally when hormones are used roots develop on the stem above the surface of the cutting medium.

Root development is usually preceded by callus tissue; in some cases this callus tissue continues to grow, developing water conducting cells but no roots. Remove any enlarged callus and treat with rooting hormone before resetting.

Before the present practice of wounding the cutting stem became common, heel cuttings were used. Heel cuttings consisted of a section of the branch with part of the stem. This provided a larger area of cambium layer to form roots and further the activity provided by the node at the base of the cutting.

Preparing Cuttings

Ensure that all equipment used is clean. Keep secateurs, knives and scissors razor sharp, and after use disinfect them with chlorine or formalin.

Never allow collected cuttings to dry out: hold cuttings in water with a few drops of hormone solution added (Hormone 20, Formula 20, Plant Hormone), and if necessary spray with water.

Carefully remove the leaves from the lower third to half of the cuttings. If the leaves are very large cut off the uppermost part of each leaf to reduce transpiration. Remove the soft tip. When mist or fog is used to propagate cuttings, longer cuttings can be used to advantage and tips need not be removed. Cut off the lower part of the stem containing the air lock, cutting below a leaf node. Wound the stem to expose an increased area of cambium layer to rooting hormone, which will stimulate it to produce roots.

The stem is wounded by removing a slice of bark and underlying tissue on one side for about 2 cm from the cut end of the stem. See diagram. Use a sharp knife, razor blade or the open blade of

wounding of cutting base

scissors. Hard matured green cuttings should be wounded on two sides.

Keep cuttings in the hormone and water solution, dipping them into a solution of 1% chlorine in water before setting into the cutting medium.

Cutting Mediums

To induce cuttings to form roots, an open textured medium which permits free air circulation and enables water to drain quickly, while holding sufficient moisture to support the cuttings, is required.

Coarse, angular quartz sand, washed to remove silt or clay, perlite, which is light and sterile, and sterilised sand are satisfactory mediums.

A little fine peat moss added to these mediums will help to hold moisture and make the medium more acid, which will encourage the development of roots. Too much peat moss holds too much moisture; this encourages fungal growth which can bring about stem rot.

When hand watering is used, 1 part peat moss to 4 parts of sand or perlite is satisfactory. With mist propagation use 1 part peat moss to 8–9 parts of sand or perlite.

Prepared medium may be acidified by watering with 1 teaspoon of malt vinegar to 2 litres of water.

Containers

Commercial growers use plastic trays which are moulded with a number of separate square or round tube-like recesses to take individual cuttings.

For general use, individual plastic tubes 35 mm in diameter and 75 mm deep are very satisfactory as they are easy to examine for root development.

Plastic pots 125 cm in diameter may be used to hold several cuttings, but root progress is harder

VEGETATIVE PROPAGATION

Cuttings prepared for cutting frame

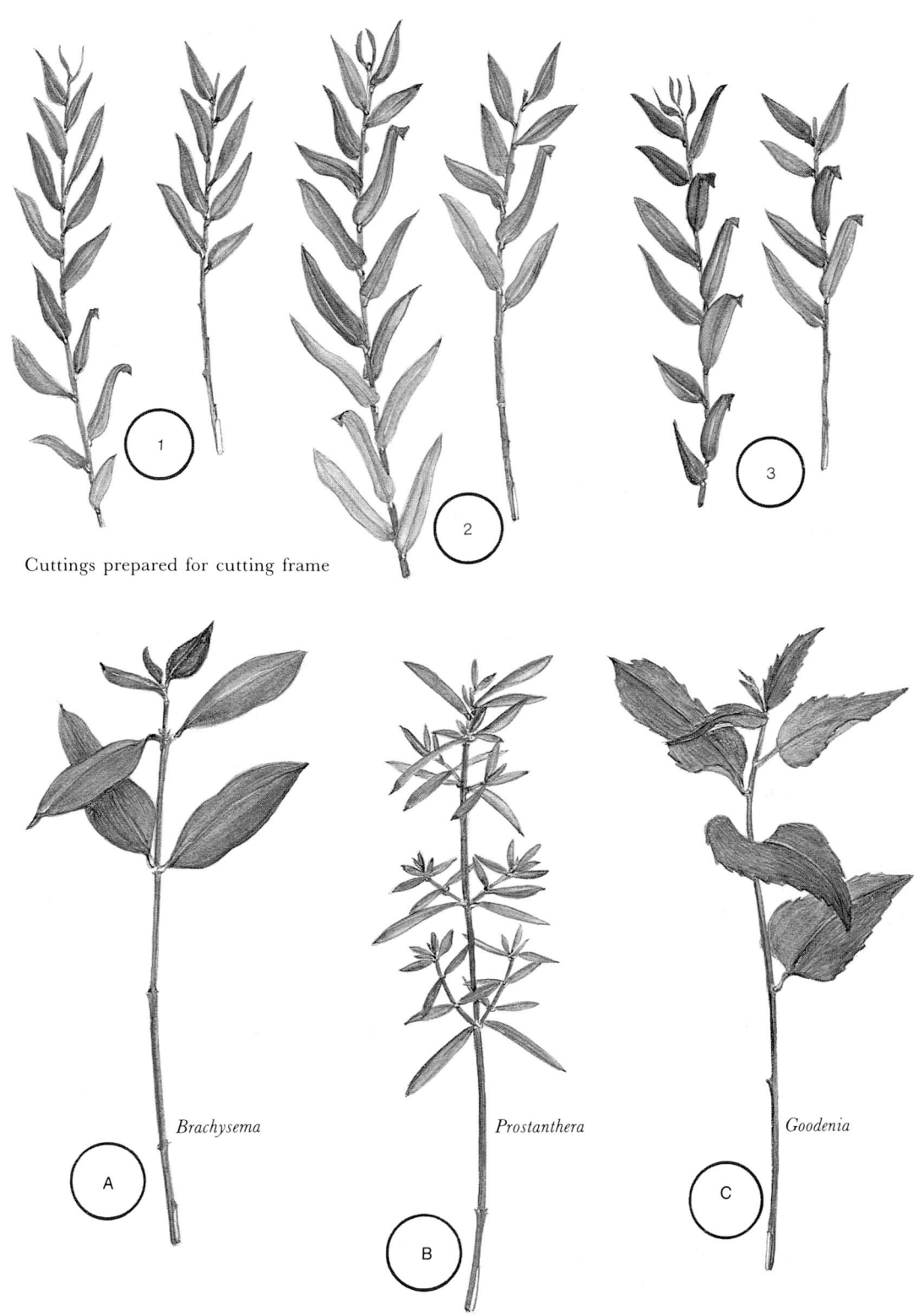

Brachysema *Prostanthera* *Goodenia*

Cuttings prepared for mist house with bottom heat (smaller than actual size)

to check and fungal attack can spread quickly to adjoining cuttings.

Also available are commercially made units of compressed peat. Round single expendable pellets, 4 cm in diameter, in which cuttings or seedlings can be placed, and multi-sectioned trays with recesses 3 cm square and 5 cm deep, which can be filled with propagating medium, are ideal. Both types of unit can be planted directly into larger containers or into the ground without removing the plant.

Cutting Enclosures

Ideal conditions for root development are provided by a saturated atmosphere at an even temperature with extended daylight.

The number of cuttings you wish to propagate will determine which of the following methods you will use to achieve a saturated atmosphere.

Glass jars
One or two cuttings may be set in a small pot of cutting medium and covered with a glass jar.

Plastic bag
For a number of cuttings a pot filled with a propagating medium may be placed in a plastic bag supported by a wire frame and tied at the top. Alternatively pull the bag over the frame and tie it around the pot.

Plastic container and bag
Place approximately 3 cm of sterilised sand in a plastic ice-cream container and set individual tubes or a community pot of cuttings on the sand. Make a suitable wire frame, and enclose the container in a plastic bag tied at the top, enabling easy access for inspection.

Cutting frames
For larger numbers of cuttings, an enclosure known as a cutting frame or cold frame may be used. A simple frame can be made using a polystyrene fruit box. Make a wire frame and cover it with clear polythene fastened on with tie-wire. Coat the polythene with whiting if the frame has to stand in full sun. Place about 50 mm of sterilised sand in the base of the box, and leave a flap at one end for easy access.

A brick or timber frame constructed on the ground is also suitable for a larger number of cuttings. A convenient size is 60 cm by 60 cm with a depth of 30 cm at the front and 45 cm at the back. Make a loose cover of glass or polythene sheeting on a wooden frame which can be opened or closed, or use two sheets of glass in a wooden frame which can be slid apart for ventilation. Coat the glass or polythene with whiting if in full sun. Place 50–100 mm of sterilised sand in the bottom of the frame.

A small propagating frame which can hold eight standard seedling punnets is available commercially. It has a plastic base and a clear moveable plastic

From left to right: cutting set under glass jar; community pot showing wire support; cuttings covered with plastic bag over support tied around the pot; plastic bag tied at top

top with adjustable ventilation openings, and a heating mat.

To use cutting frames

Place the containers with the cuttings in the frame. Keep frame closed during cold and windy days but at other times lift the covering at the back by about 5 cm to allow ventilation. Use a wooden stake placed across the frame to lift the cover; it can be moved further down if more ventilation is required. Close the frame each night. Open the ventilators of the manufactured frame during the day and close them at night.

Water cuttings once a day to ensure that they never dry out. Inspect them periodically for root development.

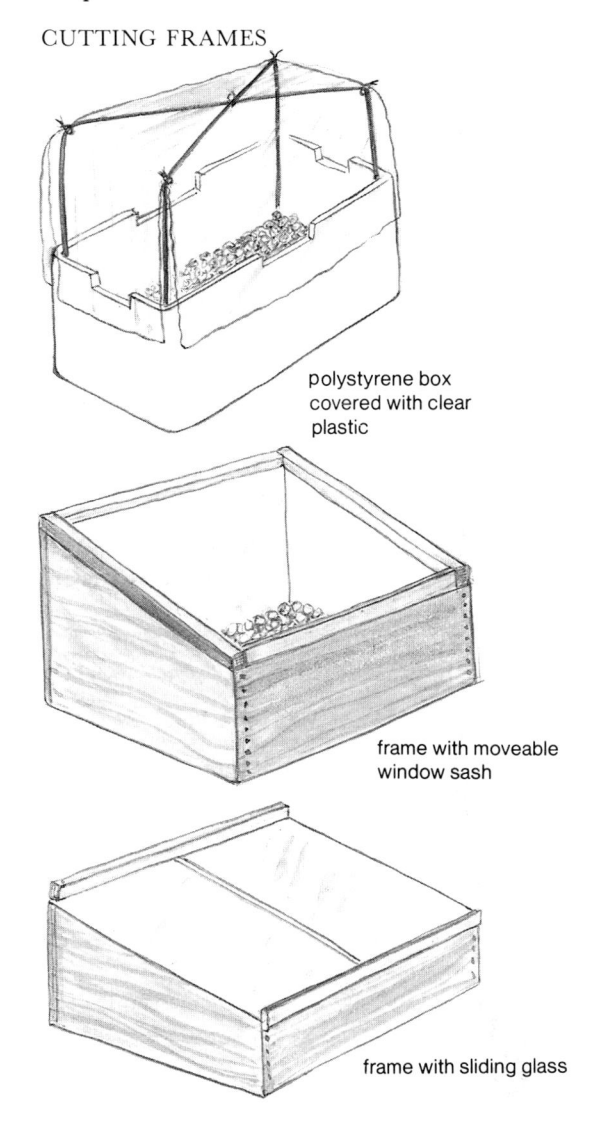

CUTTING FRAMES

polystyrene box covered with clear plastic

frame with moveable window sash

frame with sliding glass

Once a month water with Benlate fungicide at the recommended strength. Keep the frames in full sun but during hot days cover with shade cloth to prevent overheating and drying out.

Polythene or glass house

If you are dealing with large numbers of cuttings a glass house or curved frame covered with polythene sheeting provides the ideal humid atmosphere.

To cope with watering such numbers an automatic misting system is usually necessary.

Cuttings root just as readily under these conditions, but great care must be taken to prevent fungal infections spreading throughout the house. Attention to cleanliness and fortnightly fungicide spraying is essential. Bravo is recommended.

A fogging unit which adds a constant source of water as a vapour can be installed in the house. This type enclosed in a plastic tent gives good results, particularly with hirsute cuttings.

Bottom heat

Electrical resistance mats under containers will maintain a constant soil temperature between 16°C and 21°C. Heat can also be supplied from a network of pipes circulating hot water. Any heating device must be thermostatically controlled to prevent overheating. A thermometer inserted in the cutting medium is easily checked to ensure the units are working. Cuttings can literally be cooked if overheating occurs.

EXTENDED DAYLIGHT

Root development will not take place if photosynthesis is not occurring in the cutting. For quicker results artificially lengthen the day to 16 hours by providing a light source of 600 angstrom units. Use a 100-watt incandescent globe set at 91 cm above the cuttings to provide lighting for an area 91 cm square. Alternatively a 40-watt fluorescent tube set 30 cm above the cuttings will provide lighting 15 cm either side of the tube.

Control the lights by a time switch which can be adjusted as the natural day lengthens or shortens. Aim for a light period of 16 hours per day; extending the light period beyond 16 hours does not increase growth rate.

PLANT HORMONES OR AUXINS

Plants produce natural hormones or auxins, substances which regulate their growth. Research chemists have been able to artificially manufacture a number of hormones for use in vegetative propagation. The three most commonly used are IAA (indole acetic acid), IBA (indole butyric acid) and NAA (naphthalene acetic acid). They are insoluble in water and must be dissolved in ethanol (alcohol), available only to commercial users on licence from Commonwealth Customs.

For general use hormone cutting powders are made by specialist manufacturers; the hormones are dissolved and mixed with talcum powder. The ethanol evaporates, leaving the crystallised hormone on the talcum powder.

These powders are usually sold in small quantities, with numbers 1, 2 or 3 for general use; the higher numbers (4, 5 or 6) are stronger, and used by commercial growers. Very strong concentrates are used for experimental work on plants difficult to grow.

The hormones are used to aid vegetative propagation in different concentrations for different types of plants.

No. 1 (for soft herbaceous plants): 1000 parts per million.
No. 2 (for shrubby cuttings): 2000–3000 parts per million
No. 3 (for plants difficult to propagate): 8000 parts per million. Numbers 1, 2 and 3 are available in powder form in small quantities.

For commercial growers, large quantities of Nos 4, 5 and 6 are available in special concentrations:

No. 4: 16000 parts per million
No. 5: 30000 parts per million
No. 6: 45000 parts per million

Also available for general use are hormone cutting powders which contain low concentrations of IAA and NAA.

Liquid hormone substances are sometimes available from the Society for Growing Native Plants; these should be kept in a refrigerator, decanting only the required amount and disposing of any unused surplus.

A jelly-like hormone preparation, Clonex Purple, which has a concentration of 3000 parts per million of IBA in combination with other plant nutrients, gives good results with most shrubby cuttings. Use Clonex Red for harder wooded cuttings (8000 parts per million).

A liquid preparation of IAA at 5000 parts per million can give good results with proteaceous plants. This preparation should be stored in a freezer.

Access to ethanol, and accurate weighing facilities, are needed to prepare liquid hormones from hormone powders. One gram of hormone in one litre of liquid is equal to 1000 parts per million.

In a screw-top bottle mix the quantity of hormone with ethanol equal to half the amount of liquid required, and shake until the powder is dissolved. Then add the same quantity of distilled water, giving a 50% mixture of ethanol and water. To use this liquid mixture decant the required amount into a small cap and dip the cuttings in it for five seconds. Fasten the screw-top tightly and store in a refrigerator.

Only as much liquid should be mixed as will be used in the following two or three weeks.

Setting Cuttings

Overfill the planting tubes with acidified cutting medium (page 66) to allow it to firm when the cutting is pressed in. Make a hole in the centre of each tube with a skewer or stiff wire.

The prepared cuttings, which have been standing in water with a few drops of Hormone 20, then dipped in the 1% chlorine solution, are now ready for setting. Take each cutting in turn and dip into hormone cutting powder to the depth of the wound—about 2 cm—and shake off the surplus. If a liquid hormone is being used, dip the cutting for no more than 5 seconds—longer will allow too much hormone to be absorbed, burning the cutting.

Gently push the cutting into the hole, ensuring that the leaves remain free of the surface. Firm the medium around it.

When community pots are used follow the same procedure, allowing enough space between the cuttings for free air circulation.

Water well with the remaining Hormone 20 solution, and drench with water containing a fungicide such as Benlate. Cuttings propagated under mist sprays in a glasshouse are more susceptible to fungal diseases so spray fortnightly with a fungicide such as Bravo.

Never allow cuttings to dry out during the critical rooting stage. When cuttings are enclosed in a plastic bag, water only if there is no moisture showing on the inside of the bag. Usually only one watering is required during the rooting period when cuttings are grown in small enclosures.

cutting set in individual tube

Checking Cuttings for Roots

Although roots will generally develop on most herbaceous plants within a month, cuttings from shrubby types of plants may take two or three months or more.

To check individual tubes for roots watch for emerging roots or upend the tube and gently tap the base. The cutting and medium should come away cleanly; if the roots are evident the plant is ready to pot on. (Geraldton Wax cuttings should be inspected for roots within three to four weeks. If roots are allowed to become too long they can easily break off.)

If no roots are evident return to the tube, water well and leave for a few more weeks before inspecting again.

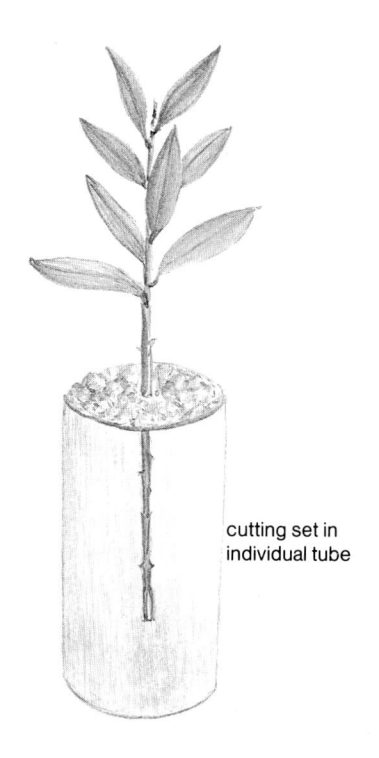

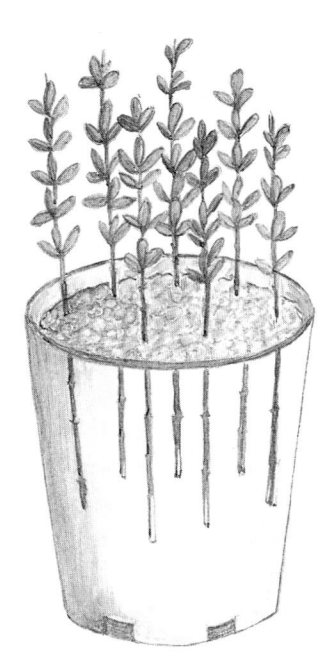

cuttings set in community pot

Cuttings in community containers can be checked for roots by gently feeling the cutting for resistance. If resistance is felt, freely water the container and gently remove one cutting. If roots are evident inspect the other cuttings by removing the container as above. If the roots are evident around the medium the plants are ready to pot on. Take care in separating the cuttings to avoid root damage.

Should few or no roots be evident return the cuttings to the container, water well and leave for a further few weeks.

Occasionally cuttings fail to root, so repeat the hormone treatment and reset, cutting off any large calluses which have developed.

Potting on Cuttings

For potting on cuttings use similar containers and potting soil as for potting on seedlings. Grow tubes 75 mm in diameter are ideal. Large containers are unsuitable as their use can lead to root rot.

Place a small quantity of soil in the container to bring the cutting to the level it was previously growing. Taking care not to damage roots, fill around the small plant with potting soil and water well. Cuttings subject to root rot, e.g. *Boronia*, should be drenched with fungicide such as Fongarid after being potted on.

Keep potted cuttings in a protected part-shaded position for about a week and then gradually expose them to full sun. Watering must be done each day.

Check for root development after about a month by upending the pot, supporting the plant and soil with one hand, and gently removing the container.

Like seedlings, cuttings are not ready for planting out in the ground or potting on into larger containers until there is good root development. Transfer potted cuttings into larger containers in the same manner as for seedlings.

Fertilizer

To keep plants growing rapidly a small quantity of a slow release fertiliser without a phosphorus content, such as blood and bone or Osmocote, may be placed on the surface of the soil after potting.

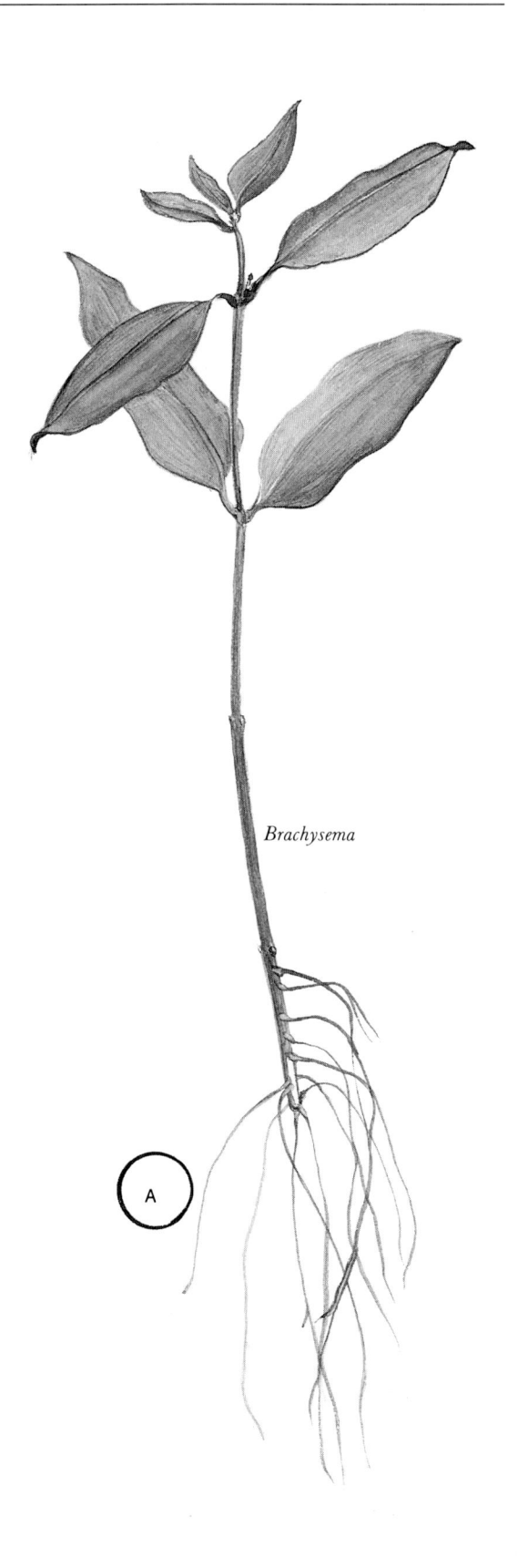

Brachysema

A

VEGETATIVE PROPAGATION 73

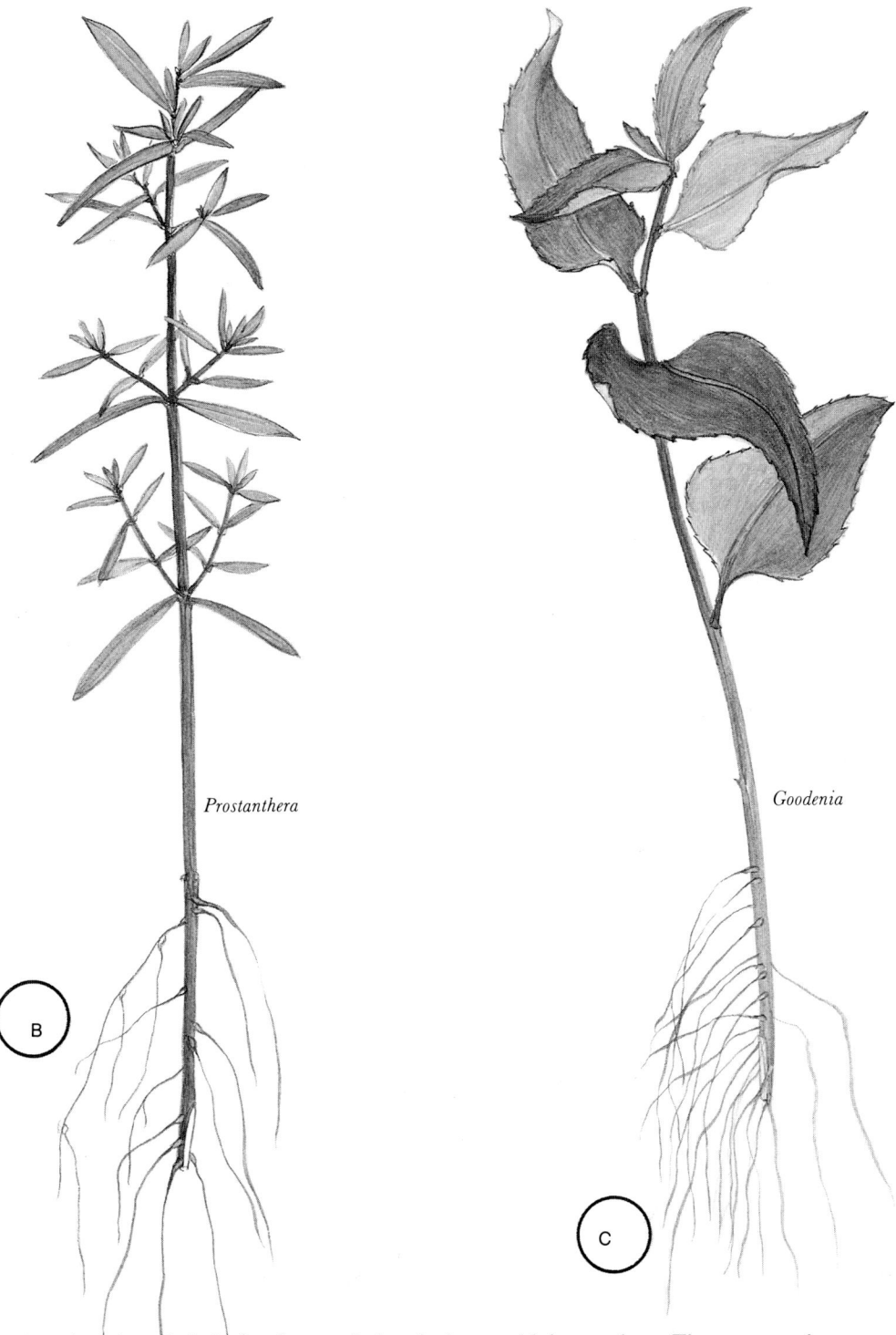

Prostanthera

B

Goodenia

C

Rooted cuttings (actual size) after four weeks in mist house with bottom heat. These appeared as prepared cuttings on page 67

LAYERING

Roots will often form naturally when a stem or leaf node touches the ground or a moist surface. This is natural layering. Plants may be induced to form roots by interrupting the normal sap flow and bringing part of the plant into contact with damp soil artificially.

All types of plants can be used for layering. Select a young, vigorous stem, make a slanting cut into it, and scrape the bark gently above the cut to expose the underlying tissue. Apply hormone cutting powder or liquid hormone to the area.

To further encourage root formation the stem is stressed by bending down and upwards into a U shape and secured into the ground. If a suitable stem is well above ground level, a pot filled with potting soil can be raised to the appropriate height.

The cut portion should be covered with soil to a depth of approximately 75 mm and kept well watered at all times.

Rooting may take three months or more. Check root progress from time to time by gently scraping away the soil.

When roots are well established sever the rooted stem from the plant and with soil still attached pot up in a suitable container, water well, and treat in the same manner as a potted cutting.

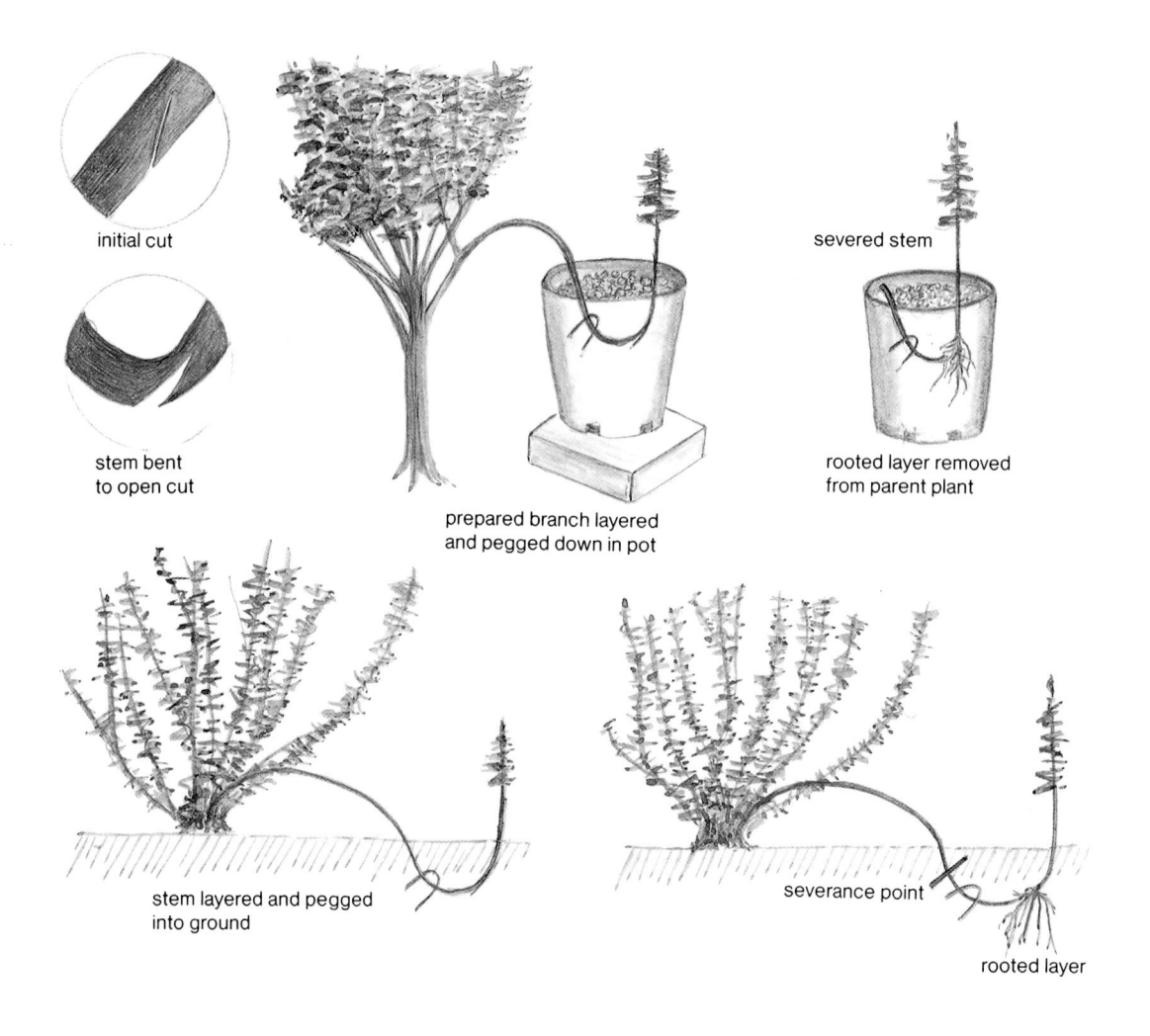

Aerial Layering

To induce roots to form by aerial layering carefully remove a ring of bark 12–15 mm wide from the stem of a suitable branch or side shoot. Gently scrape the exposed section to remove the soft tissue (phloem).

Dust the wounded area with hormone cutting powder or paint with liquid hormone. Pack a good quantity of wet sphagnum moss around the stem, wrap with clear polythene and secure at both ends with ties. Cover the plastic completely with aluminium foil, tied at both ends also.

Roots usually take three months or longer to form by this method also. Progress can be checked by removing the foil. Do not disturb the plastic covering.

When roots are well developed, cut off the rooted section and pot on into a container, water well and treat as a potted cutting. As the severed section of plant has lost the source of sap flow from the parent, extra care must be taken to ensure adequate watering is sustained and the new plant is protected until it is well established.

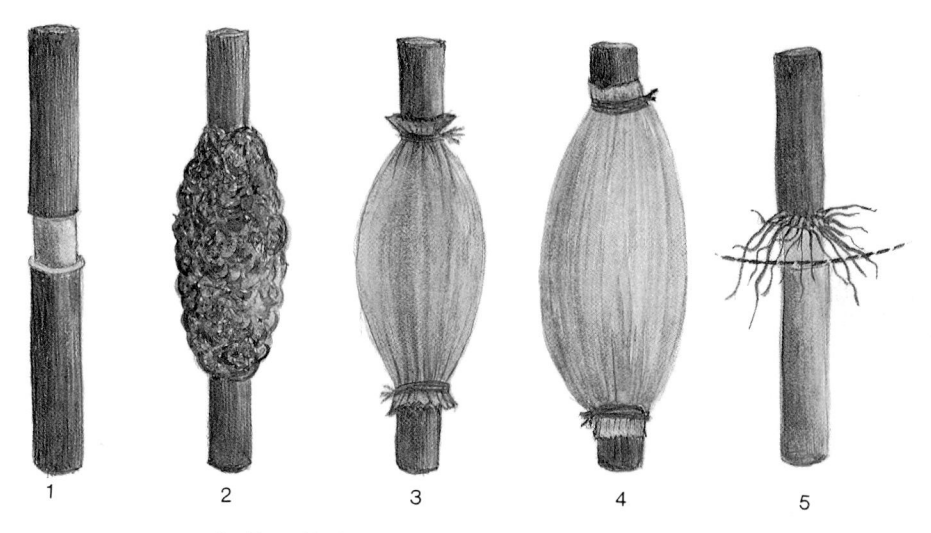

1. Ring of bark removed and phloem scraped
2. Packed with sphagnum moss
3. Covered with plastic and tied at each end
4. Covered with aluminium foil and tied at each end
5. Aerial rooted stem ready for removal

DIVISION

Perennial clump forming plants which produce new growth from underground or surface rhizomes can be divided into separate plants.

Ground covering plants such as *Viola, Mazus* and *Pratia* may be divided at any time by cutting a section of the rhizome. With soil still attached to the roots, remove the severed section from the ground. Pot on into a container, water well and treat as a potted cutting until well established.

Clump forming plants such as *Anigosanthos* can be divided in autumn or early spring. Remove the plant from the ground, wash off the surplus soil from the roots so you can see what you are doing, and divide into sections of two or three aerial stems. At the same time remove old or dead growth. Pot each section into a container, water well and grow on as a potted cutting until well established before transplanting into the garden.

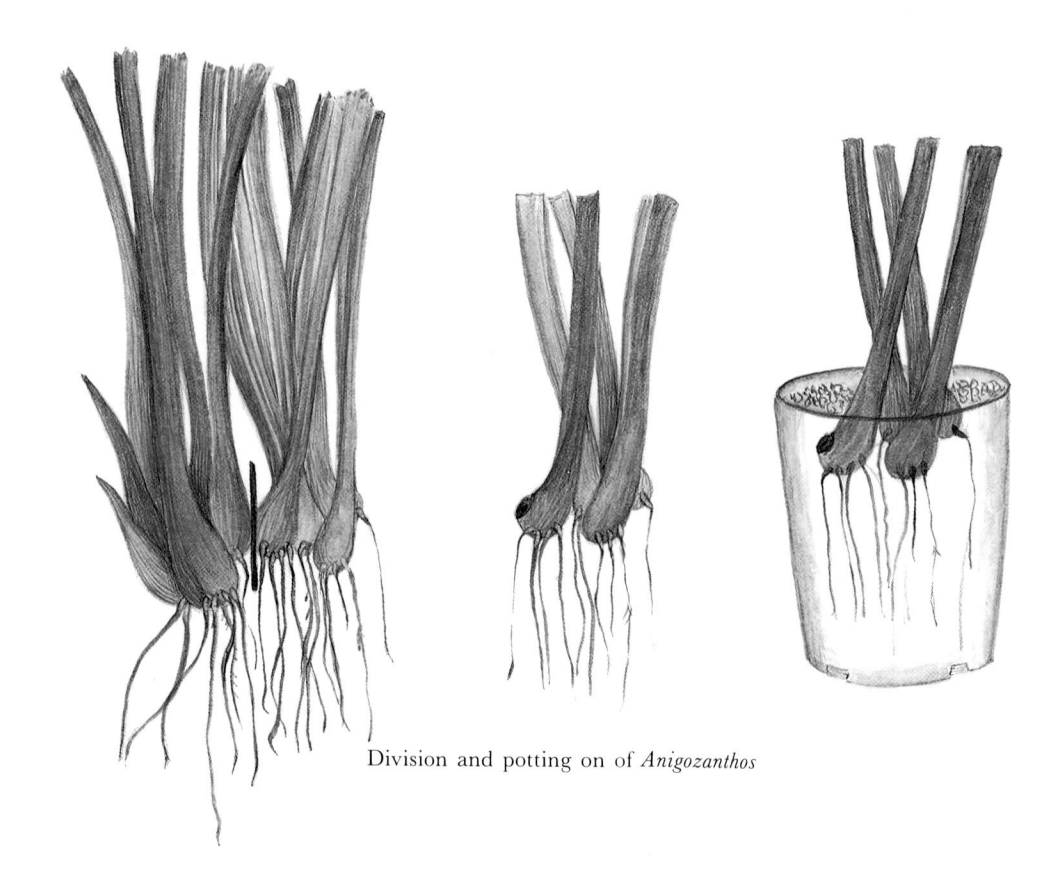

Division and potting on of *Anigozanthos*

GRAFTING

The advantages of grafting (causing a portion of one plant to unite with another) are numerous.

1. Root rot such as *Phytophthora* can be overcome by grafting disease-prone scions to resistant stock.

2. Grafting allows tropical species to be grafted onto temperate area species, enabling them to be grown in cooler southern climates.

3. Endangered specise can be increased in numbers in cultivation.

4. Various types of edible plants, e.g. *Macadamia*, are grafted with high yielding scions to improve production.

5. Exotic plants, e.g. *Camellia* with many hybrids, are grafted to the strong growing *Camellia sasanqua* root stock.

6. Plants which do not come true from seed can be grafted to maintain the variety.

7. Orchardists and grape growers use grafting to produce uniform fruit and give desirable fruiting yields. Seedlings of mangos and avocados are grafted to give desirable fruiting yields.

8. Grafted tomato plants, now readily available, provide much stronger growth and better yields.

9. New fruiting varieties can be grafted onto established trees, so changing the type of fruit previously produced.

10. Grafting can be used to repair tree stems damaged near ground level by forming a bridge with stem grafted above and below the wound.

Grafting can only be achieved with plants which have a cambium layer. The selected stem—the scion—is joined to another plant—the stock. For the graft to be successful the cellular structure of the scion and stock must be compatible; when joined the cambium layers must be in perfect alignment so that the normal function of the stem at the union can take place, allowing sap to flow to and from the leaves, building up carbohydrates in the plant, developing cellulose and forming new woody tissue.

Generally, there is tissue compatibility between species of the same genus or closely related genera. For example:

- *Westringia* is compatible with most species of *Prostanthera*

- *Grevillea robusta* and the hybrid *Grevillea* 'Royal Mantle' are compatible with many *Grevillea* species

- *Banksia integrifolia* and *B. ericifolia* are compatible with many Western Australian *Banksia* species. *Banksia integrifolia* is also compatible with some *Dryandra* species

- *Myoporum* species are compatible with some *Eremophila* species

- *Thryptomene saxicola* is compatible with some *Verticordia* and *Calytrix* species

Sometimes an apparently successful graft will suddenly die, but unfortunately the reason for this is not yet fully understood.

A problem with Australian natives is that although a grafted plant may grow well the developing buds can be pushed off before the flowers open, evidently due to the stronger growth of the stock plant. To counteract this problem with the stock plant *Westringia fruticosa* and the scion plant, the small *Prostanthera aspalathoides*, the Canberra Botanic Gardens have successfully used a small piece of *Prostanthera nivea* between them. This has the effect of reducing the sap flow to the grafted plant.

Six year old specimen of the prostrate *Grevillea* 'Royal Mantle' grafted to the main stem of *Grevillea robusta*

VEGETATIVE PROPAGATION

When to Graft

For the most consistent results in grafting, it should be done at a time when the stock plant is growing actively and the scion has buds which are just swelling, but not in active growth. Scions are selected as if they were being chosen for semi-hardwood cutting material (page 64).

The scion should be no larger in diameter than the stock plant stem. If the scion has a smaller diameter than the stock plant, one side of it should be aligned with one side of the stock plant.

The scion should have two or three nodes and be long enough to make the graft. Large leaves may be cut or a number removed to reduce transpiration. To further reduce transpiration, the grafted scion should be covered until union occurs, using a large glass jar, a plastic soft drink bottle with the base removed or a supported plastic bag. The covered grafted plant should be kept in a well lighted glasshouse or a protected position and watered regularly.

(To overcome the problem of transpiration one Queensland member of The Society for Growing Australian Plants removes the leaves from the scion and binds both graft and scion with a thin plastic laboratory film, Parafilm® or Nescofilm®, through which developing shoots emerge.)

When the graft has taken and the growth is established the covering should be removed for longer periods each day.

Making the Graft

If you have no experience in grafting we suggest you practice cutting, fitting and binding two pieces of stem together until you have mastered the technique. A small spring clip taken from the back of a commonly used conference name tag is very useful in holding the two pieces together.

Speed in carrying out the grafting operation leads to success, so have all the materials you need gathered together—potted stock, scion material, knife, plastic grafting tape or grafting film. The knife must be razor sharp and cuts made with a single stroke.

Remove the leaves from the vicinity of the graft, make the grafting cuts and immediately place the two cut surfaces together to prevent drying out. The grafted material must then be kept in intimate contact at all times and handled with care to prevent the two surfaces being disturbed.

Tying the graft

Raffia, covered with grafting wax, was used for tying before the advent of plastic grafting tape, which is impervious to moisture. Tie the plastic tape tightly below the graft and bind around the stem to just above the graft, overlapping the tape to ensure the graft is kept in intimate contact. Tie off by slipping the end under the previous turn of the tape.

When the grafted scion is producing new shoots, the tape is carefully cut and removed.

As the diameter of the stems used in grafting native species is small, the thin stretchable and self adhesive clear plastic laboratory films called Nescofilm® or Parafilm® are ideal. A new type, Biograft, incorporates a fungicide. Thin strips about 10 mm wide are cut from the end of the film roll. The plastic film is gently stretched and bound around the grafted areas as before, overlapping and gently pulling tight at the finish. The film can be left on after the graft has taken as it stretches easily and does not restrict plant growth, although it may be removed if you prefer.

The union of the graft under good conditions may be as quick as ten days or may take a month or more. The plant must be handled with care while the union is still soft. When the plant is growing well, remove all leaves and shoots below the graft. Ensure dormant buds beneath the graft do not develop later on.

When a side graft is made below the top of a stock plant, the upper part should be cut back in stages after the scion is growing vigorously.

Top Wedge Graft

This type of graft is the simplest for small stemmed plants. Cleanly and squarely cut across the stem of the stock plant below a node and make a vertical cut 10 mm deep in the centre of the stem. The scion is also cut cleanly across, then each side of the stem cut to form a wedge which when pushed into the stock covers the cut area, ensuring the cambiums are in alignment. The two pieces are then tied together with plastic tape and the plant covered with a glass jar or plastic bag until the scion is growing well. Remove the cover for a longer period each day. The plastic tape may also be removed.

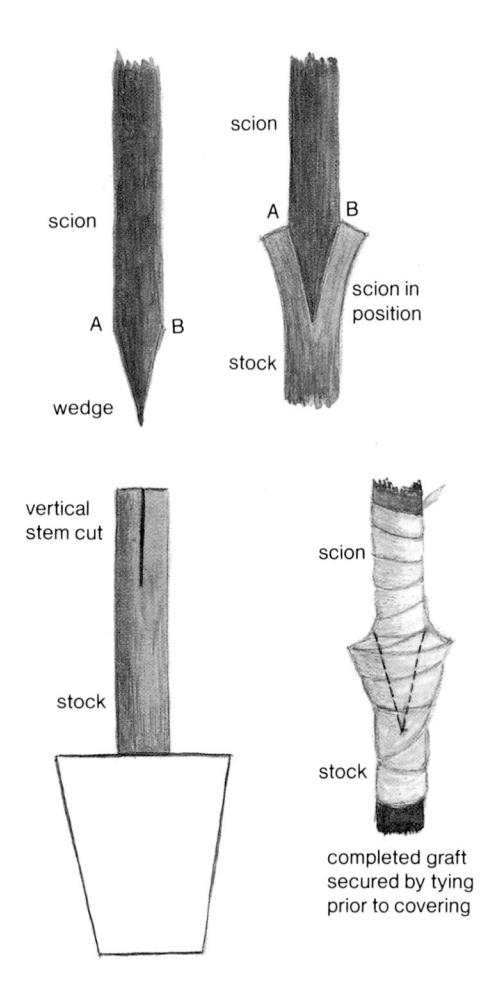

Top Wedge Cutting Graft

With species of plants which root readily from cuttings, cuttings can be used as stock plants. Prepare the stock cutting, about 75 mm long, by removing lower leaves, wounding and treating with rooting hormone. Cut off the top and make a slit down the middle to a depth of about 10 mm. The scion, about 50 mm long, with lower leaves removed for about 15 mm, is then cut on both sides to a wedge shape. Push the pieces together and tie with plastic film. The cutting with graft is now ready for setting. If set in a glasshouse under mist conditions a jar should be placed over the cutting to reduce fungal problems.

When the upper grafted section is growing and the cutting is rooted, remove the glass jar for longer periods each day until the cutting is well established.

Carefully pot on in the usual manner.

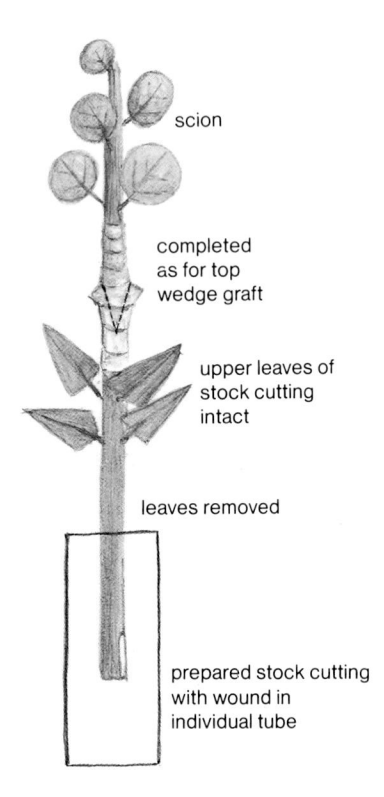

Top Wedge Cotyledon Graft

In this form of graft two seedlings are grafted together in their early stages of growth. As the seedling stems are tiny and soft, this method requires great skill, patience and care.

The stock seedling is cut off just below the cotyledon and a vertical cut is made in the stem. The scion seedling is cut off below the cotyledon and above soil level with enough length to form a small wedge and allow for tying with film after fitting together. Place a glass jar over the seedling until growth is well established on the scion.

Side Wedge Stub Graft

In this type of graft a sloping cut is made into the stem of the stock plant to a depth of about 15 mm. The scion is cut on both sides to form a wedge which is completely pushed into the cut on the stock plant. The grafted section is then tied with plastic film, ensuring that the junction is airtight. Cover the plant with a supported plastic bag.

When the scion is growing strongly and is well established the section of stock plant above the graft can be cut back gradually to just above the union.

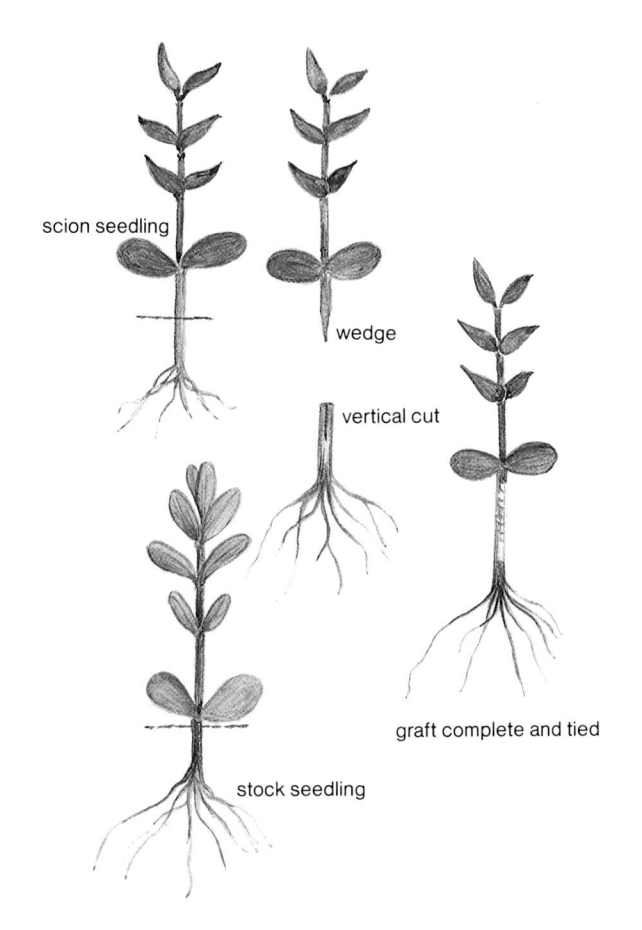

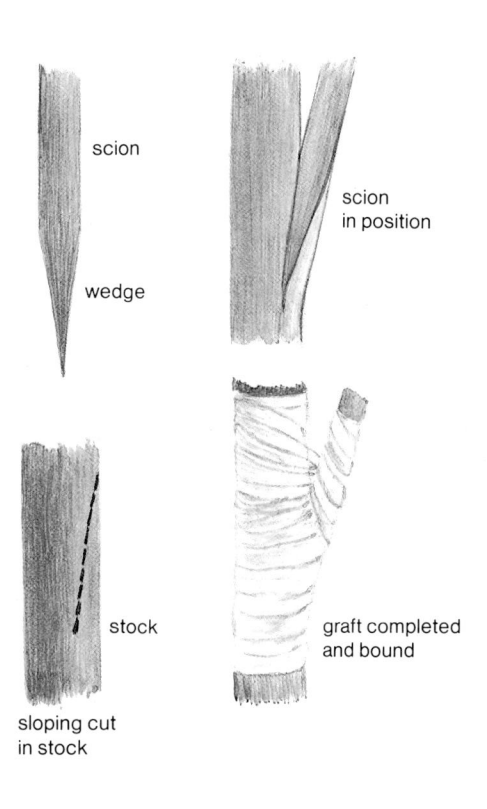

Top Whip Graft

In this graft the stock plant is cut cleanly across and then a sloping cut made on the stem to a length of about 2 cm. A matching cut is made to the scion and the two pieces are bound together with plastic tape ensuring that the two cut surfaces and the cambium layer match perfectly. After tying the grafted section is covered with a jar or supported plastic bag and placed in a glasshouse or a well lighted protected position.

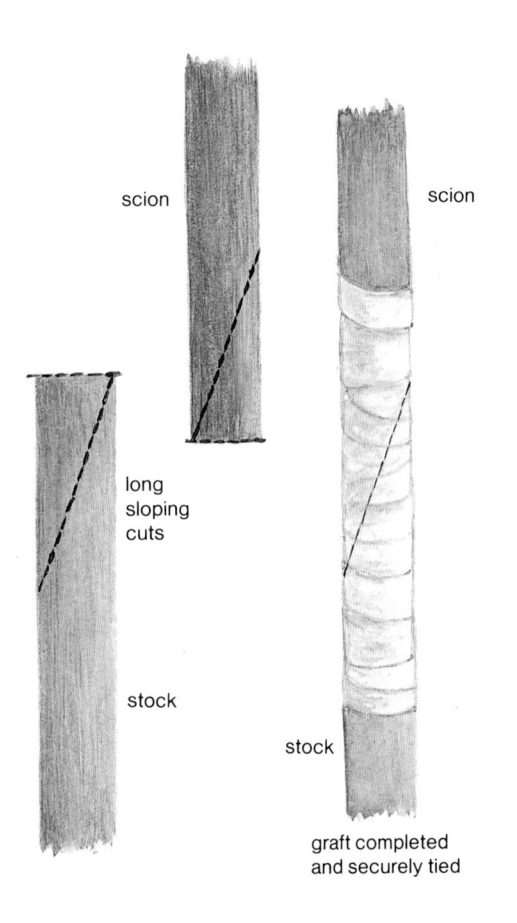

Top Whip and Tongue Graft

This graft is considered the strongest of the top grafts and is widely used in grafting deciduous fruit trees.

It requires great skill in cutting and fitting the tongues of the two pieces together. The union in the centre of the tongue results in a better deposition of new tissue which gives a stronger graft.

Cleanly cut across the top of the stock plant. Make a sloping cut about 2 cm deep down the stem, as for the whip graft, then make a vertical cut in the stem about one-third from the top, forming a tongue. The scion is cut in a similar manner and the two tongues are pushed gently into each other, matching the cambium layers. Bind the graft with plastic tape, and treat as other grafts until well established.

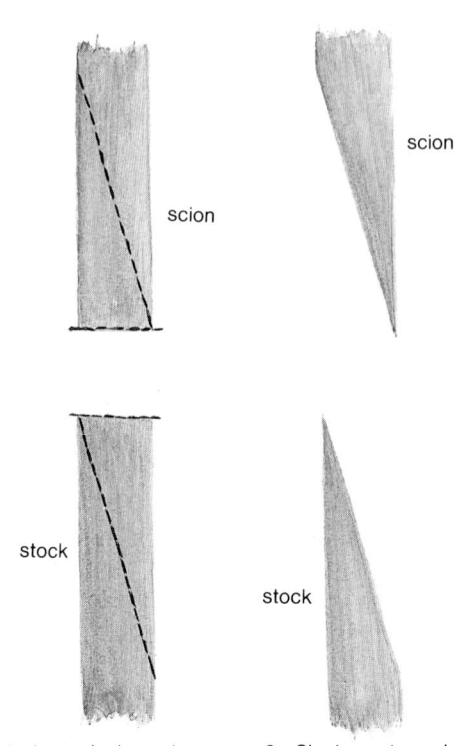

1. Long sloping cuts   2. Sloping cuts made

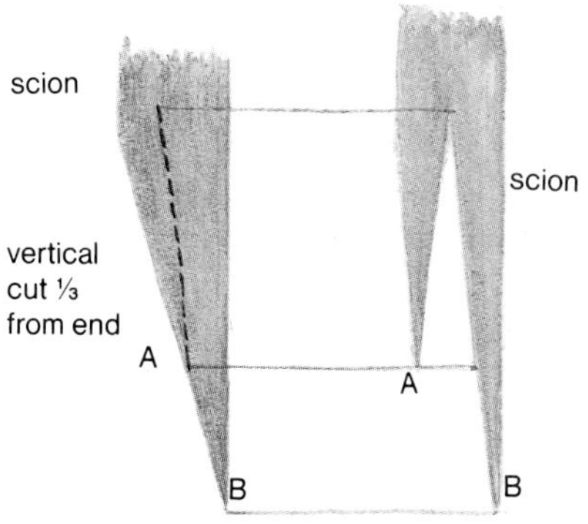

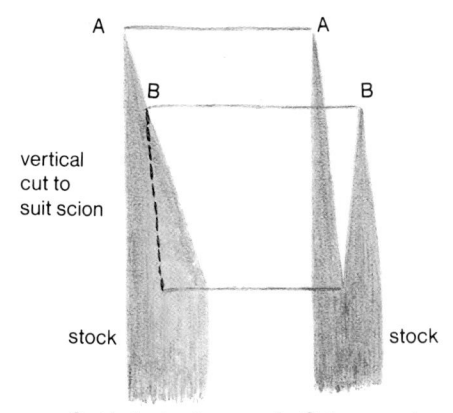

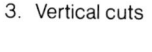

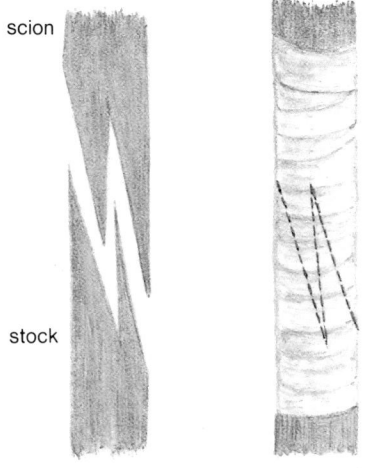

Side Whip and Tongue Graft

In this graft a shallow downward cut is made in the side of the stem to about 2 mm deep. A sloping downward cut is then made, commencing about 2 cm above the 2 mm cut. A second vertical cut is made about one-third from the top of the sloping cut to form a tongue. The scion then has a sloping cut made to match that of the stock plant and a vertical cut is made one-third from the end to form a matching tongue. The two pieces are gently placed together, tied with plastic tape and treated as other grafts until the graft is established. When the scion is well developed the stock plant above the graft is reduced in stages to just above the graft.

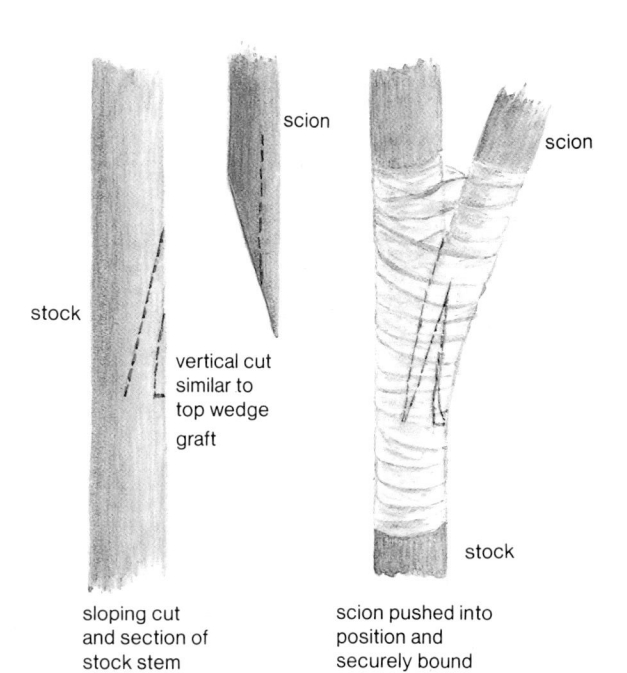

BUDDING

Budding is joining a single bud to a stock plant. It is widely used in rose growing, for joining buds of selected roses to strong growing briar stock. Budding is also widely used in the citrus industry, joining single buds to strong-growing stock plants of *Poncirus trifoliata* and the bush lemon.

T Budding

T budding can only be carried out where there is a strong enough flow of sap to allow the bark to be lifted from the underlying tissues.

As the bark of most Australian native plants is not readily parted from the underlying tissues the use of T budding is restricted.

Make a horizontal cut through the bark only on the stock plant, then a vertical cut, forming a T. Loosen the bark from the stem. Cut a firm, plump bud from the selected plant, gently ease it into the T cut, and bind with plastic tape. When the bud is growing strongly slowly remove the section of the stem above the bud.

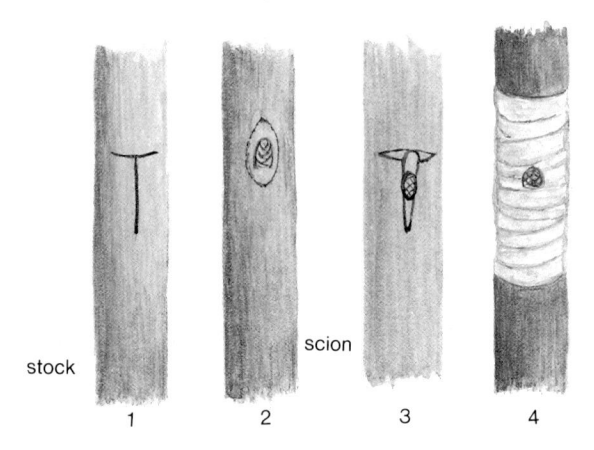

1. T cut in stock plant
2. Bud removed from scion plant
3. T cut opened, bud slipped into position
4. Bud securely bound with film

Chip Budding

In this form of budding, make a horizontal downward cut to a depth of about 3 mm on the stock stem and then a sloping cut beginning about 15 mm above this cut to connect with it. Remove the slice or chip. Select a plump dormant bud from the desired plant and cut it away to match the slice, ensuring the longer sloping cut is just above the bud. Slip the chip bud into position and completely cover, binding with plastic film. The growing bud will eventually emerge through the film. It is not necessary to enclose this budded section with a jar or bag during union. When the bud is growing strongly and is well developed, slowly remove the stock plant in sections to just above the bud.

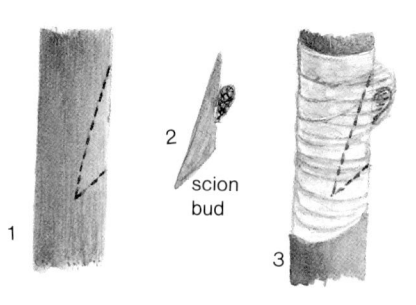

1. Chip removed from stock stem
2. Bud and chip removed from scion plant
3. Chip in position and bound with film

Patch Budding

Select a plump, dormant bud on the plant which is to be joined to the stock plant. Make horizontal cuts 1 cm above and 1 cm below the bud, then a vertical parallel cut on each side of the bud, and gently remove the bark and bud. Make matching cuts into the bark on the stock stem and remove that section of the bark. Insert the bud patch, ensuring that it is tightly fitted. Bind with film and treat as for chip budding. The bud will eventually emerge through the film.

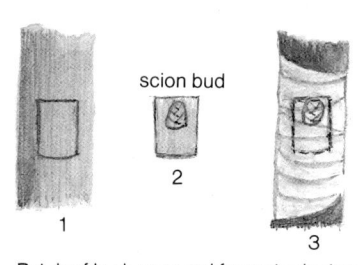

1. Patch of bark removed from stock stem
2. Patch of bark with scion bud
3. Patch inserted and securely bound with film

VEGETATIVE PROPAGATION   85

Top wedge graft showing union between stock and scion *(Photo courtesy Peter Abell)*

Whip and tongue graft showing union between stock and scion *(Photo courtesy Peter Abell)*

Whip and tongue graft tied with Parafilm®

Potted *Dendrobium* species growing in bush-house

Early development of protocorms—symbiotic

Close up of small protocorms with orchid roots at 3 months—symbiotic

Protocorms beginning to develop leaf—symbiotic

Close up of protocorms with developing leaf—symbiotic

Advanced *Dendrobium* seedlings growing asymbiotically in a flask

Dendrobium seedlings developed naturally among orchid roots

8 Orchid Propagation

Australian orchids follow similar patterns of reproduction to the exotic species. With both groups, raising orchids from seed is a very slow process and requires patience. Vegetative propagation is generally readily achieved by following the methods outlined.

PROPAGATION FROM SEED

Keep the orchid fruit under observation and collect the seed in a clean paper bag or envelope as the fruit begins to split. To ensure the seed is kept free of moisture add a small packet of silica gel (found in tablet bottles), seal, label and store in a dry position.

Sow seed as soon as possible, as fresh seed gives the best results. (Provided it is kept dry, seed can be stored in a refrigerator for a limited period.)

Germinating Seed Symbiotically—Method I

Epiphytic orchids
There are a number of epiphytic orchids, but only a few genera are generally cultivated. *Dendrobium* species and their many hybrids are the main group, as well as species *Sarcochilus* and their many hybrids, *Bulbophyllum*, species of *Liparis* and limited cultivation of the beautiful *Phalaenopsis, Vanda, Oberonia* and *Cymbidium*.

Select a well grown pot of orchids with a vigorous root system, preferably of the same genus as the seed to be sown.

Water the pot well and sprinkle the seeds around the roots. Gently spray the seeds with a fine mist, and keep the orchid in a well protected part-shaded position. The seed on and around the surface of the roots should be kept moist at all times, but be careful not to overwater and wash the fine seed away.

Within a month or two, tiny green onion-like growths should appear among the roots of the host orchid. A very weak solution of fertiliser such as Aquasol or Zest can be given at three-monthly intervals. Allow at least another twelve months for development, or until two small leaves appear on the tiny bulbs, before pricking out.

Fill a small seed punnet with a mixture of equal parts of peat moss, fine granular charcoal and casuarina or fir bark. (If *Pinus radiata* bark must be used, first soak in in lime water for a week and then wash well with boiled water.) Water well.

Make holes in the mixture and prick out the seedlings, firming around each plant. Water well with a weak solution of Aquasol and Hormone 20; also apply a weak solution of fungicide such as Benlate. Keep the seedlings in a sheltered position in a polystyrene box covered by a sheet of glass. Water regularly.

When the seedlings are growing well gradually remove the glass covering and transfer them to individual 50 mm pots filled with the same seedling mixture. Keep the small pots in a protected bushhouse or glasshouse.

Fertilise every two weeks with the weak Aquasol and Hormone 20 solution, watering well in between times to wash away excess salts.

Allow the small plants to grow on until the pots are filled with roots. Using granular charcoal as a growing medium, transfer the small seedlings to 75 mm pots. Fertilise every month with a dusting of dry poultry manure. Ample watering must be maintained.

When the plants have filled the pots with new growths, transfer them to 100 mm pots, still using granular charcoal as a growing medium. Water regularly and ensure the pots drain freely.

By keeping the plants growing well flowers should appear in six or seven years. By using extended light, such as fluorescent light, to supplement daylight to 16 hours a day, flowering can be achieved within four years.

Continue to fertilise the orchids for vigorous growth, potting on into larger containers and watering freely.

Pests such as snails, grasshoppers and Dendrobium beetle can be kept at bay with snail baits and an insecticide spray such as Malathion.

Terrestrial orchids

Growing terrestrial orchids from seed is more difficult. Some success can be achieved by using a cultivated pot of terrestrial orchids, sowing similar seed on the soil surface and keeping moist in a protected shady position, taking care not to overwater.

Small seedlings may develop but as the growth of these plants first takes place underground, it is impossible to assess their initial development.

GERMINATING SEED SYMBIOTICALLY—METHOD II

Epiphytic orchids

This is often known as the old towel or Turkish-towel method.

Strict conditions of cleanliness must be adhered to when using this method to prevent infection of the spores by fungi. Use thin disposable gloves when working and wear a mask.

Soak for one hour in a 10% chlorine solution the equipment needed:

- A clean knife.
- A 100 mm terracotta or plastic pot with matching saucer.
- A piece of glass large enough to overlap the pot.
- A piece of clean white towelling 10–12 cm square.
- A mixture of hard fern fibre, sphagnum and peat moss compacted to about the size of a cricket ball, wrapped in a piece of clean cloth.

Wash a suitable working area with the same chlorine solution, before washing the pot, saucer, glass and towelling in boiled water to remove the chlorine solution. Immediately cover the pot with the glass.

Wash the fibre ball with boiled water before wrapping it in the towelling square and placing it in the pot. Push the sides of the towelling down into the pot with the clean knife. Fill around the sides of the ball with sphagnum moss which has been washed in cold boiled water. Sprinkle the seeds over the towelling and cover with the glass immediately.

Cut a number of 2–3 cm tips of orchid roots, preferably of the same genus as the seed, and wash in cold boiled water. Put the orchid roots among the seeds on the towelling. Gently water the pot with cold boiled water, allowing surplus water to fill the saucer (this water level must be maintained) and immediately replace the glass.

If the seed is fertile, a spider-like web of hyphae from the fungus in the roots will develop over the seeds and towelling in about four to six weeks. The hyphae will grow into the tiny seeds and in another month or two the seeds will develop into tiny colourless onion-like growths, known as protocorms. These protocorms will eventually develop chlorophyll, becoming green, and develop fine hair-like root outgrowths.

protocorms (enlarged)

protocorms with chlorophyll and developing leaf

protocorms with first leaves and root hairs

protocorms developing into small plants with roots

Orchid roots among seed on towelling with sphagnum moss between towel and pot. Covered with glass.

From the apex of the protocorm a small leaf will emerge. When this leaf is well developed the tiny seedlings may be fertilised with a small amount of liquid fertiliser, such as Aquasol, dissolved in cooled boiled water at 1/20th of the recommended strength. Use an eye-dropper to apply this weak solution among the small seedlings. Use the same strength to fertilise the seedlings every three months.

When a second leaf has formed on the seedlings, about twelve months after sowing, the seedlings may be hardened by removing the glass for lengthening periods, extending the time until it can be finally removed. Prick out the seedlings and pot into a community tray or punnet, using the same potting mixture and procedure as in the first method (page 87). When the seedlings are growing well, transfer them to individual 50 mm pots filled with the same mixture. Keep the small pots in a protected bush-house or glasshouse. Water with boiled water only, fertilising fortnightly and treating once every three months with a very weak solution of fungicide such as Benlate.

Use pieces of charcoal, free from dust, for the growing medium when plants are large enough to be potted on into 75 mm containers. Fertilise with a light dusting of dry poultry manure or liquid fertiliser and water daily.

Flowering should begin after six to eight years, depending on rate of growth, and providing vigorous growth is maintained flowering should occur each year.

Plants can be continually potted on into larger containers.

Terrestrial orchids

The problem of germinating terrestrial orchid seed was solved by a horticultural researcher at the Canberra Botanic Gardens, who isolated five groups of fungi associated with them and developed a technique to culture the isolated fungi for an indefinite period.

To germinate the seed, using aseptic conditions and a low nutrient medium, the seed is sown and then inoculated with the appropriate fungus. The developing plants are allowed to grow on in the medium until ready for transplanting.

Unfortunately the isolation and cultivation of the various fungi is a highly specialised process beyond the scope of most orchid growers.

developing growths which have shed leaves

Seedling orchid at first flowering stage

Germinating seed asymbiotically

In the asymbiotic method the seeds are germinated without the presence of a mycorrhizal fungus. The asymbiotic germination of orchid seeds was developed in 1922 by an American, Lewis Knudson, who was of the opinion that if the nutrients required by the seed could be provided it would be possible to germinate the seed without the presence of the mycorrhizal fungus which supplies these nutrients in nature. Knudson published a chemical formula necessary to achieve the results. The Knudson C formula, with some modification, is still in use:

Calcium nitrate, $Ca(NO_3)_2.4H_2O$	1.00 g
Monobasic potassium phosphate, KH_2PO_4	0.25 g
Magnesium sulphate, $MgSO_4.7H_2O$	0.25 g
Ammonium sulphate, $(NH_4)_2SO_4$	0.50 g
Ferrous sulphate, $FeSO_4.7H_2O$	0.025 g
Manganese sulphate, $MnSO_4.4H_2O$	0.0075 g
Sucrose, $C_{12}H_{22}O_{11}$	20.00 g
Agar	12.15 g
Distilled water	1 litre

Unless facilities for accurately weighing the ingredients are available, and large numbers of seeds are to be dealt with, it is better to obtain prepared mixes from specialist dealers.

Keep all substances in airtight containers as they readily absorb moisture from the air.

To prepare the formula mix, bring distilled water almost to boiling point and stir in the powders until they are dissolved. The pH should be approximately 5.8. This may be adjusted with the use of hydrochloric acid.

The seeds are sown in clean glass flasks with rubber stoppers. A glass tube inserted through the stopper should be filled with sterile cotton wool. If using jars, special plastic covers, also with a glass tube filled with sterile cotton wool, should be used.

Pour the formula mix to a depth of about 12–18 mm into each container. To produce faster growing seedlings, the formula can be changed by replacing 10% of the water with young fresh coconut milk and adding a few slices of ripe banana.

Sterilise the containers and covers in a laboratory autoclave at 170°C for 30 minutes. A pressure cooker may be used for sterilisation but to ensure complete sterilisation the process must be repeated a day or two later.

Seed sowing should be carried out in a dust-free atmosphere to reduce contamination. A fishtank, or a wooden-framed box covered with clear plastic with a loose flap for the opening, is suitable. Both must be washed with a strong chlorine solution before use. (Commercially, seed sowing is done in a flow chamber in which filtered air is blown from the chamber towards the operator.)

Soak the seed for 20 minutes in a solution of 5 grams of calcium hypochlorite to 70 millilitres of sterilised water. Remove the seed and wash well in sterile water.

Using plastic gloves washed in a chlorine solution, and wearing a mask, pass the top of each flask or jar over a bunsen burner flame and place the containers in the chamber. Form a small loop at the end of a piece of platinum wire or tungsten wire (from an incandescent globe).

To sow the seed pass the wire loop through the burner flame, pick up the seed with the loop and spread it over the agar mix in the containers. Replace the stoppers and ensure the containers are kept in a well lighted position. A fluorescent light positioned about 30 cm above the containers for a period of 16 hours a day will speed up the growth.

Within a few weeks the tiny seeds gradually enlarge, forming small onion-like protocorms, which develop chlorophyll and turn green. Fine hair roots will form and the apex of the protocorm will extend; after about six months, a small leaf will develop. Wait until the second leaf develops before transplanting.

(If the containers become contaminated with fungi, loss of the small seedlings may result; if the seedlings have developed a leaf, they may be transplanted from the contaminated container onto wet sterilised sphagnum moss, watered with a weak solution of Aquasol and Benlate fungicide and covered with a plastic bag.)

Prepare small punnets with a mixture of peat moss, sphagnum moss, small pieces of charcoal and casuarina bark or fir bark and saturate with boiled water (see page 87).

To transplant the small seedlings from the flasks or jars use the looped wire and remove each one in turn. Gently wash the agar mixture off each seedling with warm water (body temperature), place them in small holes made in the mix and firm around each seedling.

Water the punnet with a weak solution of Aquasol and a fungicide such as Benlate. Place in a polystyrene box covered with a sheet of glass, removing it only for watering, and keep in a cool, well lighted position. Water daily with a fine spray and fertilise monthly.

After one week spray the seedlings again with a weak solution of fungicide (Benlate) and then at three monthly intervals.

When the seedlings become larger and new leaves develop the glass cover should be removed for short periods until it can be fully removed. Watering must not be neglected and during hot weather the small plants should be sprayed twice a day.

As the plants grow larger, they can be transplanted into individual 50 mm pots, using the same potting mix. After transplanting, spray with a fertiliser and keep them in a protected, well lighted position and water daily.

When the small pots become full of roots transplant the seedlings into 75 mm pots in a medium of pieces of dust-free charcoal and sprinkle lightly with poultry manure at monthly intervals. Keep the plants well watered.

A soluble fertiliser may be used as a spray as an alternative to poultry manure.

As the plants are grown on, transplant into larger pots, filling the pots with extra pieces of clean charcoal.

Seedlings of pendulous forms of orchid, e.g. *Dendrobium teretifolium*, can be transplanted from the 75 mm pots to pieces of cork bark, seasoned hardwood or sections of treefern bark, tying firmly with strips of nylon stocking. Water once or twice daily and fertilise by spraying monthly.

Dendrobium falcorostrum seedling at first flowering stage, developed naturally (symbiotically) on trunk of *Banksia serrata*. This eight year old plant has received daily watering

VEGETATIVE PROPAGATION

Vegetative propagation is readily carried out with many species of orchids following the methods discussed here.

Dendrobium Orchids

Species with very short rhizomes and erect stems
In *Dendrobium* new stems usually develop from the base of an existing stem. (These erect stems are often wrongly termed pseudobulbs.)

During the growth of the new stems flower buds develop at the apex and often in the axils of the upper leaves. New growth must be vigorous and flower buds must form within it, as they will not form at a later stage. During the next flowering season, the buds may produce an inflorescence, usually from the apex, and sometimes from both apex and leaf axils, e.g. *Dendrobium kingianum* and its hybrids. (In *D. speciosum*, flower buds on the new stems usually take two years to form inflorescences.)

Flowering often occurs over two or more seasons from the same stem. When the buds are exhausted, the leaves usually fall, and sometimes for no apparent reason the stem dies.

In a well grown plant a new growth commonly develops from the base of the flowering stem and sometimes from other stems at the same time.

Other small plants may develop from a flower bud at the apex or from the buds on the stem and form roots.

Branches develop from the rhizomes of creeping species, e.g. *Dendrobium lingueforme*, with short-stalked fleshy leaves developing from them. Depending upon the vigour of the growth, one or more flower buds, which usually flower the following season, may form in the leaf axils.

Roots develop from the rhizome, attach and spread over the surface on which they are growing.

Species with erect stems
Dendrobium orchids with erect stems may be divided into several sections, whether they are growing in pots or on a surface. Allow the plant to dry out for a few days, then remove any small developing plants on the stem and pot them on.

Frequently plants with well grown, well aerated root systems will have roots attached to the side of the pot. Knock the plant from the pot or carefully apply pressure to ease it out. If all else fails, break the pot. Where orchids are attached to a surface, gently ease the roots from the edges until the orchid is free.

When you divide an orchid, you should have at least three or four stems in each new section, as a number of basal shoots will enable the section to re-establish readily.

Using a very sharp knife carefully cut into the rhizome, taking care to avoid the lower buds on the stems. Gently pull the part-severed section from the plant and remove any dead or damaged roots and stems. For about an hour, soak the divided section in water with a small quantity of Hormone 20 added.

Use a pot slightly larger than the piece of orchid. While holding the plant below the top of the pot fill around it with pieces of charcoal, pressing firmly around the roots.

Hold the pot under running water to ensure drainage holes are unobstructed.

Dust the surface of the pot with dry poultry manure at monthly intervals and water well. As an alternative to poultry manure a fertiliser such as Aquasol may be used at fortnightly intervals, but daily watering is needed to remove excess salts. Keep plants in a well lighted protected position.

Orchids may be grown on a group of rocks placed directly onto the ground. Make a space for the orchid and fill firmly around it with pieces of charcoal. Apply a small quantity of dry poultry manure and water well.

Orchids can also be grown on trees which do not shed their bark, e.g. *Melaleuca*, on sandstone boulders, seasoned hardwood or cork. Tie the orchid tightly to the surface with a strip of nylon stocking, cord or wire. Sandstone rocks can be drilled and plugged and nails used to fasten the ties to hold the orchid securely. Large orchids such as *Dendrobium speciosum* may be kept tight against a flat rock using extra stones as weights. Ties may be removed when the orchid roots are attached to the surface.

Orchids growing under these conditions require more frequent watering and fertilising than potted orchids—and remember to take precautions against pests.

ORCHID PROPAGATION 93

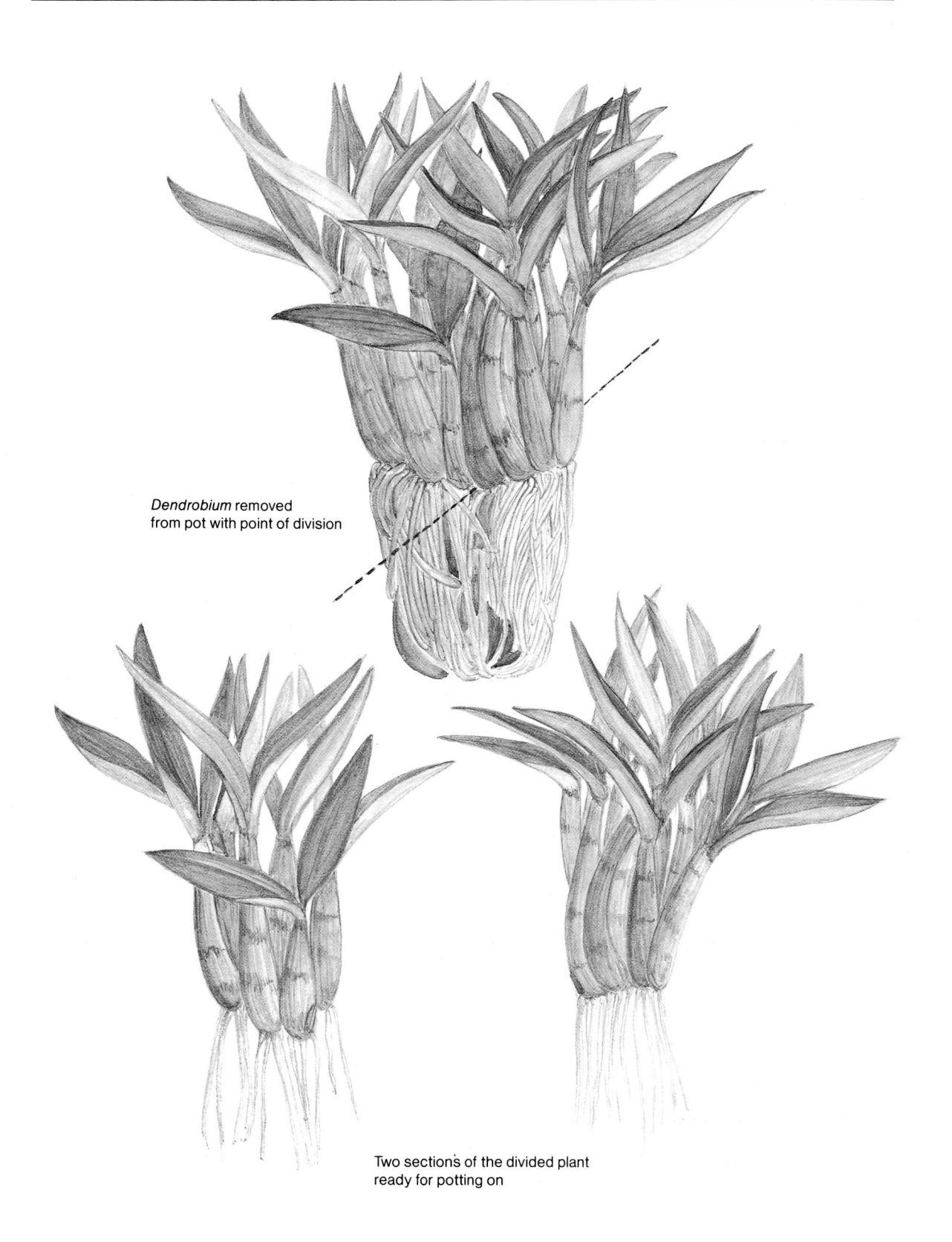

Dendrobium removed
from pot with point of division

Two sections of the divided plant
ready for potting on

Aerial plants

Dendrobium species with erect stems frequently form small plants from the stem—these are known as aerial plants or keikis. Allow these small plants to develop roots before removing them and growing on as separate plants.

Creeping species

Dendrobium, Bulbophyllum and other species with similar patterns of creeping growth may be divided when the rhizomes become large enough or multibranched.

Allow the orchid to dry out for a few days. The rhizome of the section with several branches is then cut and gently eased from its growing surface. Remove all dead leaves and damaged roots before soaking in water with a small quantity of Hormone 20. Attach the orchid to a surface—a piece of seasoned hardwood, cork bark, a tree which doesn't shed its bark or to a piece of sandstone, and treat as described on page 92.

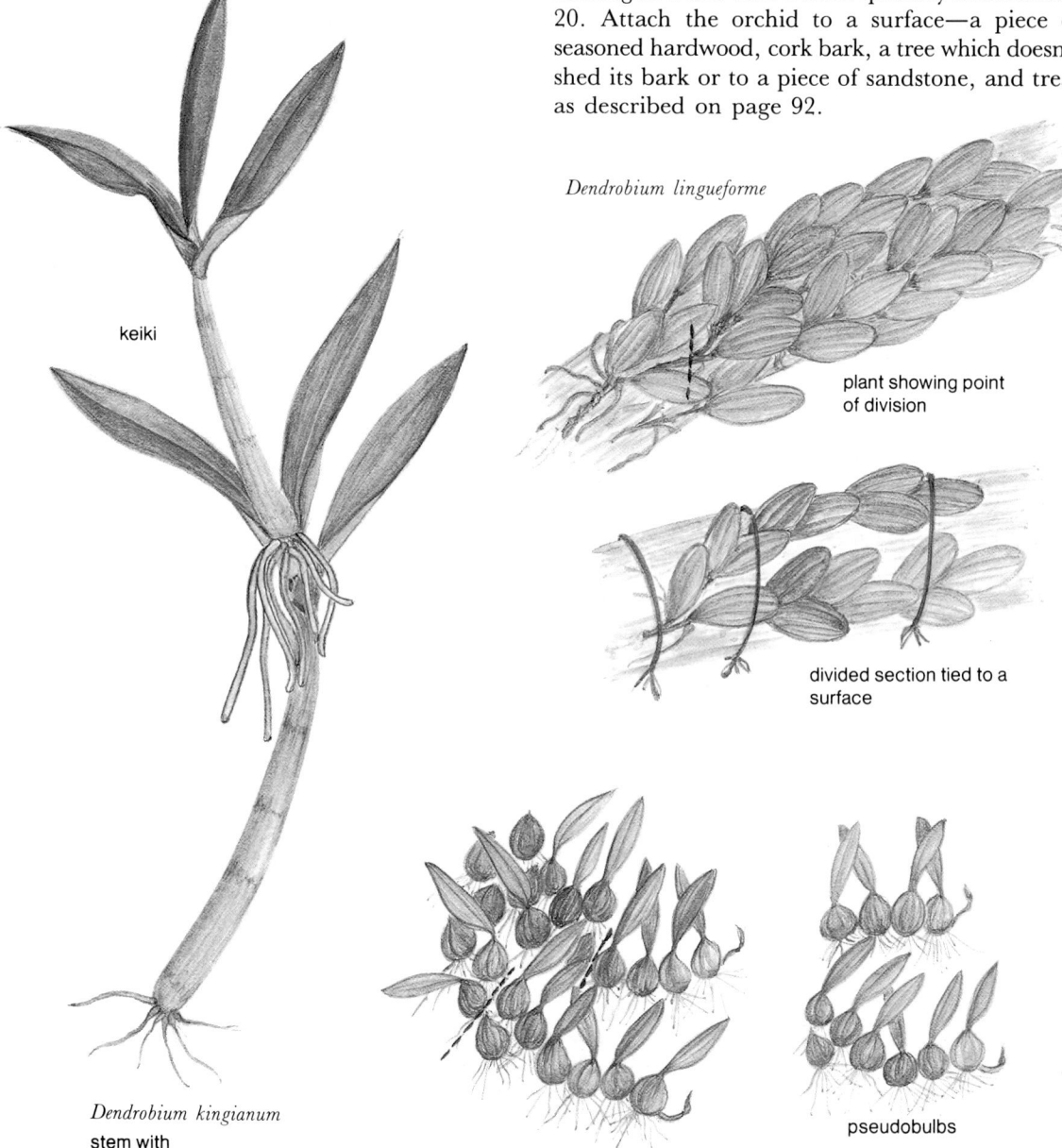

keiki

Dendrobium lingueforme
plant showing point of division

divided section tied to a surface

Dendrobium kingianum
stem with developed aerial plant ready for removal

Bulbophyllum exiguum
points of division and divided sections

pseudobulbs

ORCHID PROPAGATION

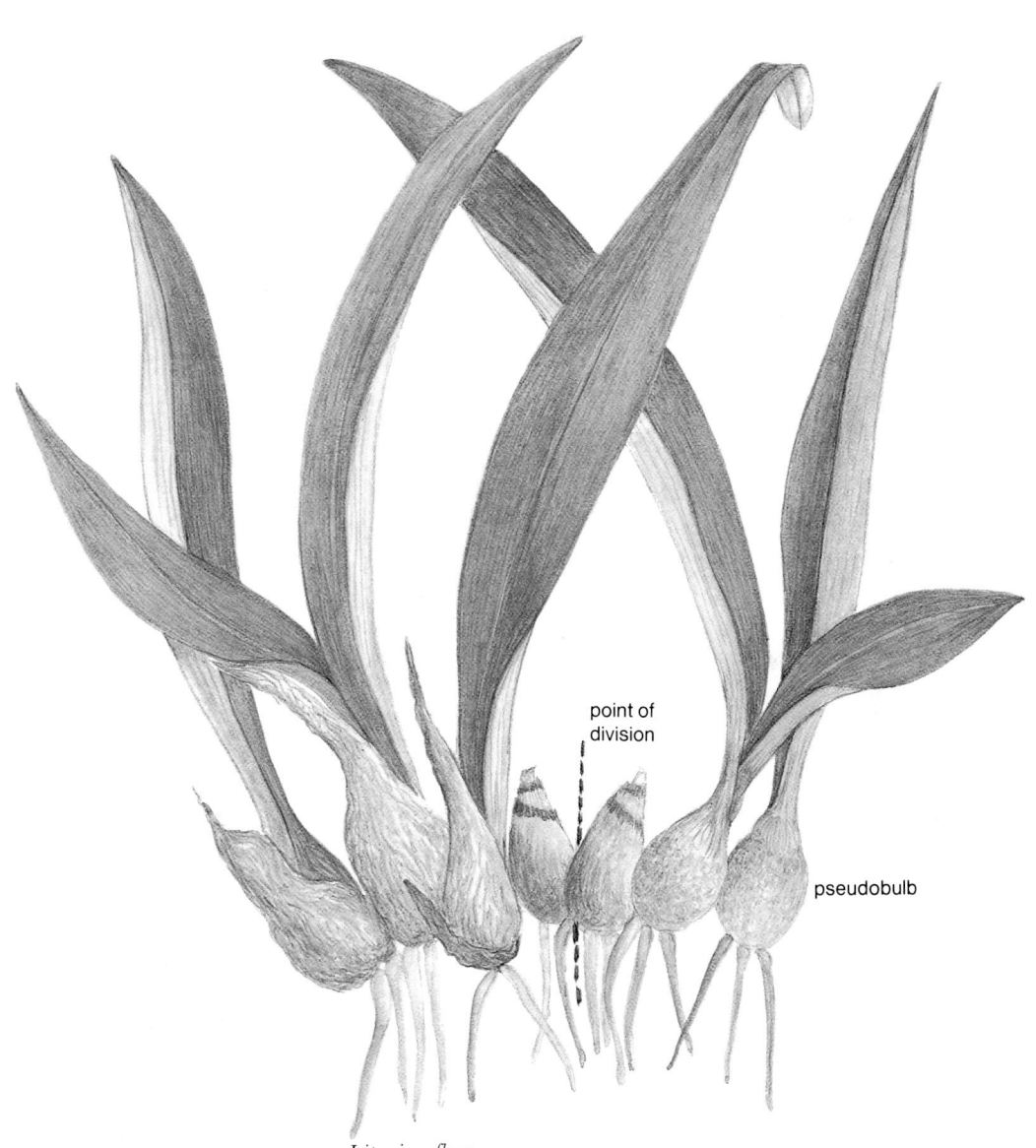

Liparis reflexa

Pendulous orchids

To divide orchids such as *Dendrobium teretifolium*, tie the pendulous stem back to a moist surface of sphagnum moss. This induces the plant to produce roots from the stem. The rooted section can be cut off and tied to a suitable surface. As the area which is attached to the new host is small, drying out can be rapid, so watering must be on a regular basis, at least once daily. Cover the roots with sphagnum moss to aid their attachment to the surface. Fertilise monthly.

Some small terete-leafed orchids, e.g. *Dendrobium striolatum*, develop rooted sections without assistance. Remove and soak in water with a small quantity of Hormone 20. Attach to a new surface as before.

These orchids can be grown successfully in wire baskets lined with shade cloth and filled with a mixture of charcoal, peat moss and casuarina bark, with a small quantity of poultry manure added.

As with other orchids, daily watering is essential.

rooted section divided for removal

two sections divided

Dendrobium striolatum

Dendrobium teretifolium

Cymbidium Orchids

These orchids have a growth habit intermediate between epiphytes and terrestrial species. Epiphytes attach themselves to the surface on which they grow by their roots. Terrestrial species grow in the ground. *Cymbidium* orchids grow in the hollows of trees with roots extending deeply into the decayed wood inside the tree.

There are three Australian species of *Cymbidium*. Two of them, *C. canaliculatum* and *C. suave*, resent disturbance and propagation by division. Although, like exotic Cymbidiums, *C. canaliculatum* has swollen pseudobulbs at the base of each leaf it is still very difficult to cultivate. *C. suave* has slender stems which extend in length as the plant matures and produces new stems but is still difficult to divide.

Cymbidium madidum has large pseudobulbs making it possible to divide two or three pseudobulbs from the parent plant and is more obliging than the other two when it comes to propagation.

Allow the plant to dry out, knock it from the pot, divide and remove any damaged roots. Soak for an hour in water containing a small quantity of Hormone 20 and pot on into 200 mm containers or a hollow log, using standard Cymbidium potting mix.

After potting, water well and fertilise with Aquasol at three monthly intervals. Keep the plant in a well lighted position in a bush house.

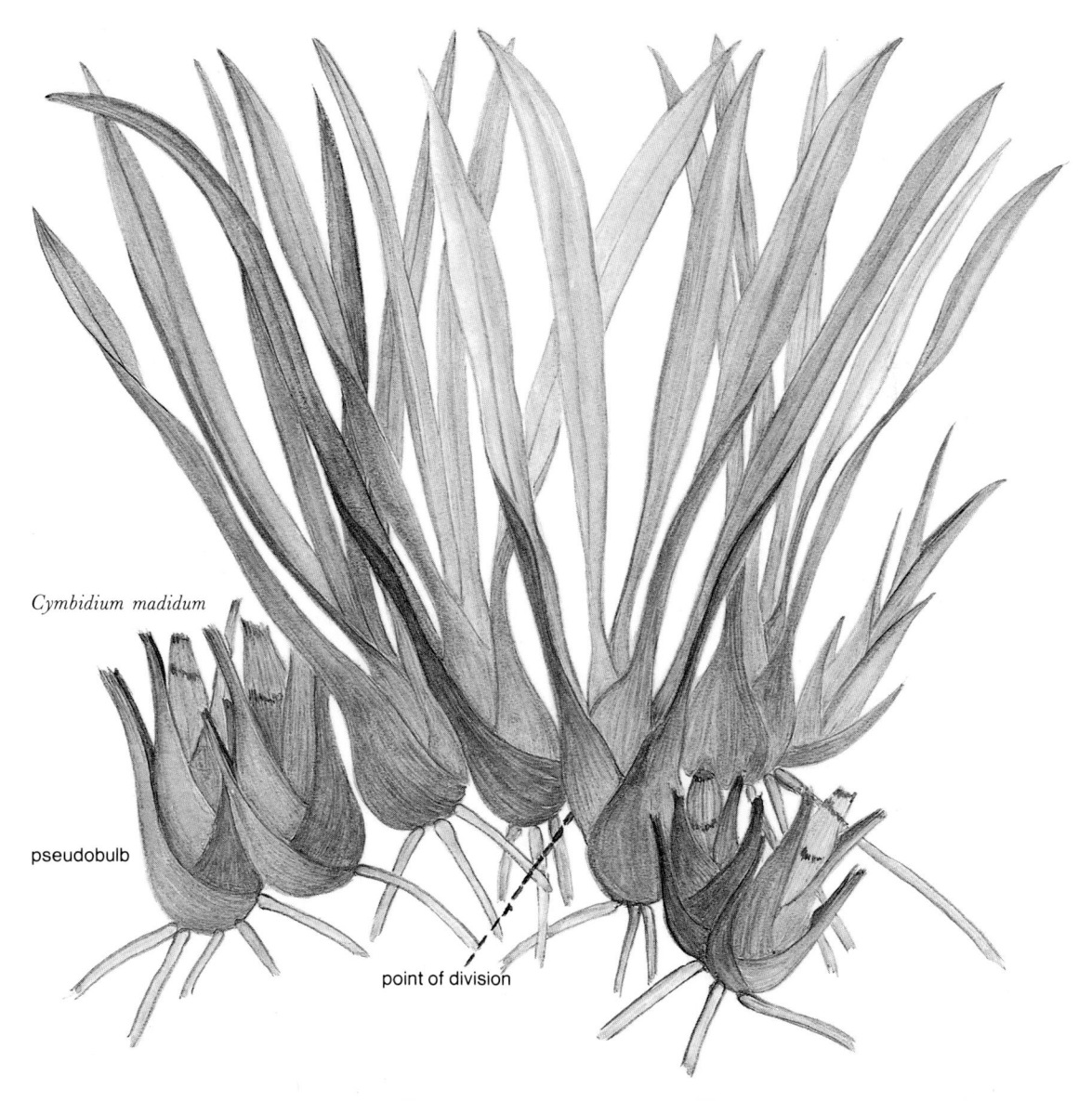

Cymbidium madidum
pseudobulb
point of division

point of division

Sarcochilus fitzgeraldii

The Subtribe *Sarcanthinae*

Many genera from this group require specialised treatment in cultivation. The propagation methods used here are confined to the genus *Sarcochilus*.

Many species of this genus do not form branches, which would make division easier, and thus need specialised propagation treatment. In some species it is possible to induce branching by removing the growing tip of the plant, but with others such a practice is doomed to failure.

The roots of these plants are long and fleshy and often grow free. Species such as *Sarcochilus fitzgeraldii* and *S. hartmannii* and their many hybrids form small branches, sometimes called keikis or aerial plants, which develop fleshy roots.

These aerial plants can be removed and cultivated as separate plants. To propagate, cut the aerial stem through, leaving it in position until it is growing well. Then carefully remove the section from the parent plant, cut off any damaged roots and leaves and soak in water containing a small quantity of Hormone 20.

Pot on into a well drained shallow container using a mixture of pieces of charcoal, peat moss and casuarina or fir bark in equal quantities. Hold the plant in position in the pot and fill firmly around the roots with potting mixture. Water well and spray with a fertiliser such as Aquasol.

These orchids like a moist atmosphere and plenty of light, but not direct sunlight. Water daily and fertilise monthly. When grown on a surface such as cork bark or the surface of a tree they need continual attention. The addition of sphagnum moss over the roots will assist in holding moisture.

S. fitzgeraldii divided section ready for potting on

Terrestrial Orchids

Some Australian species of terrestrial orchids are evergreen, while others produce new growth from a small potato-like underground tuber or tuberoid each year, flower, seed and die down. Some species of *Pterostylis* and *Caladenia* form branching underground rhizomes or roots, producing a new tuberoid at the end of each branch. Each tuberoid forms a new plant, making a community of separate plants during the next season. The majority produce only a single tuberoid which is renewed each year. Given suitable conditions new plants develop from seed. In their natural state colonies at varying stages of development may be found.

The evergreen terrestrials have fleshy leaves and roots, e.g. *Spiranthes, Cryptostylis, Phaius* and *Calanthe*.

Spiranthes forms a single stem (sometimes branching) arising from fleshy roots. The seed of this species germinate readily among other orchids.

Cryptostylis forms clumps by branching of the short rhizome.

Phaius and *Calanthe* form pseudobulbs from which arise large fleshy leaves and thick fleshy roots.

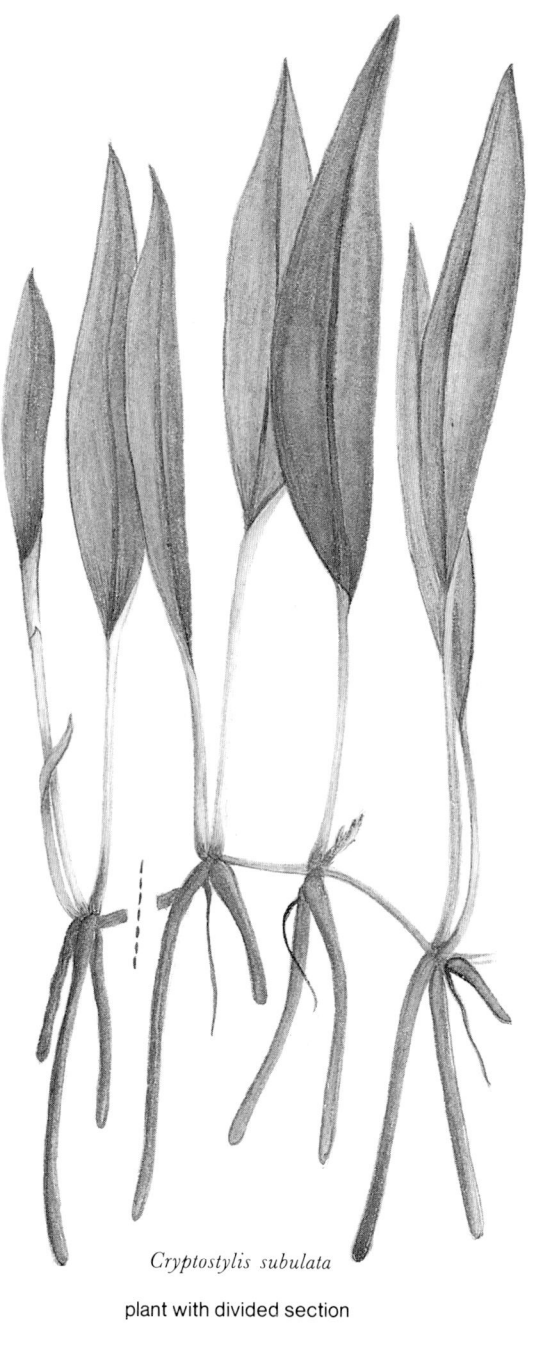

branch plant with point of division

branch plant removed

Spiranthes sinensis

Cryptostylis subulata

plant with divided section

Tuberoid Species

Pterostylis nutans, P. curta, P. baptistii and *Caladenia catenata*, all with underground tuberoids, form colonies and can be propagated.

When the plant dies down, usually in December, sort out the small tuberoids and transplant them into a well drained plastic pot, 100–125 mm in diameter, nearly filled (3 cm from the top) with a mix of:
  50% quartz river sand
  20% sphagnum moss
  30% coarse eucalypt mulch

Place four to six tuberoids on the mix and cover to a depth of 2 cm. Water well and keep medium damp, remembering that the tuberoids will rot if the medium is too wet. Place in a protected area in 60% shade. When the new growth appears, water daily and spray with a liquid fertilier once a month.

Plants may be left in the same container for two years before they need repotting.

Species which make only one tuberoid each year can be knocked from the pot and checked for the formation of an additional tuberoid which may be grown on as a separate plant. Do not mistake the old shrunken tuberoid for a new one.

These species may be left in the same container and mulched each year with eucalypt mulch.

Experiments with *Diuris punctata* tuberoids has met with some success. Cut the tuberoid in two with a razor blade through the growing tip, and place each half in potting mix. Allow the two halves to grow on, when a new tuberoid may form on each half.

Small Evergreen Species

Evergreen terrestrial species such as *Cryptostylis* which form rhizomes can be divided. Select a section of the plant with three or more leaves and cut the rhizome during the growing period. Wait until the cut section is growing well before removing and potting on in a separate container using the potting mix above. Water well and regularly and spray with a weak fertiliser such as Aquasol once a month. Place in a protected position with 60% shade.

Spiranthus sinensis usually grows as a single plant but sometimes branches and forms a second plant which can be divided by cutting the rhizome and soaking it for an hour in water with a small amount of Hormone 20. Plant in a mixture of peat moss and sphagnum moss in a small container with or without drainage holes. Water well daily and spray with a weak solution of fertiliser every three months. Keep in a well lighted protected position.

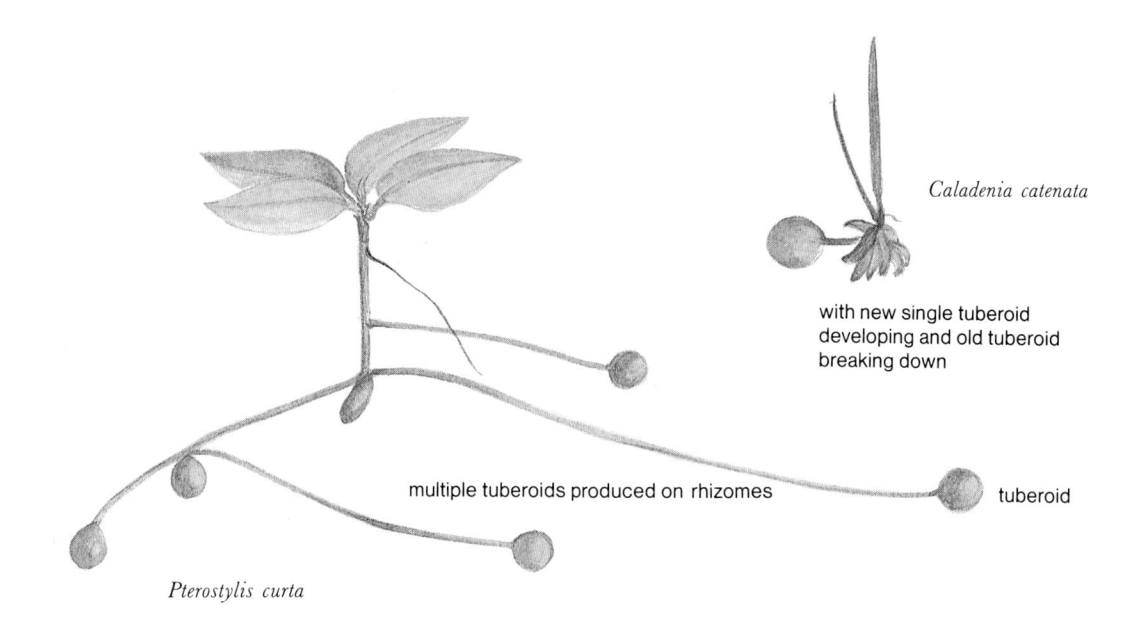

Caladenia catenata

with new single tuberoid developing and old tuberoid breaking down

multiple tuberoids produced on rhizomes

tuberoid

Pterostylis curta

Large Evergreen Species

The genera *Phaius* and *Calanthe*, with large pseudobulbs, have similar habits of growth and can be divided.

Allow the plant to dry out before knocking it from the container. Cut two or three pseudobulbs from the main plant, removing any damaged roots and soaking the section for about an hour in water containing a small quantity of Hormone 20.

Pot into a large deep container using a medium of:
- 40% coarse sand
- 20% leaf mould
- 10% peat moss
- 20% rice hulls

Add to a 10 litre (2 gallon) bucket:
- 20 grams of 9 month slow release fertiliser (Osmocote or Nutricote)
- 10 grams of dolomite

Phaius requires a well lighted position but *Calanthe* should be kept in 60% shade. Take precautions against pests.

Calanthe triplicata

point of division

pseudobulb

Potted *Dendrobium* orchids in author's bush house

Dendrobium orchids growing on rocks in author's garden

Early development of *Pellaea falcata* prothalli

Close up of developed prothalli

Prothallus with first frond developing

Punnet of small *Cyathea cooperi* ferns

9 Fern Propagation

Raising ferns from spores is a very slow process. Vegetative propagation, however, can give rapid results.

Ferns differ from flowering plants in having spores for reproduction instead of seeds. In seeds there is an embryo which contains the primary roots and leaves of the new plant, whereas in ferns the spores must go through a slow sexual stage before young plants develop.

PROPAGATION FROM SPORES

Under suitable conditions of moisture and temperature spores released by the sori on fertile fronds germinate and form a prothallus, which at first is slender, and by cell division develops two lobes, ultimately forming a heart or shield shape. The two lobes are a single layer of cells in thickness. In the upper middle of the shield an area called the cushion develops, which is several cells thick. On the upper surface of the lower part of the lobes antheridia, male organs, develop; on the upper part of the cushion archegonia, female organs, develop. On the underside of the cushion and from the lower edges of the lobes fine hair-like roots (rhizoids) develop.

The mature antheridia burst on the top to release sperm cells. Providing there is an adequate film of water, in completely humid conditions the sperm cells will swim to the female archegonia. If the archegonia are mature fertilisation occurs and small ferns develop.

The development of ferns from spores is a slow process, varying with the different species, and may take from a few months to twelve months or more. The germination of some spores is very difficult and may even be impossible for those species which require an association with a particular mycorrhizal fungus.

Spores may be infertile, perhaps because they were immature at the time of collection or were not fresh when sown.

fertile frond

sori on pinnule

spores

developing prothallus

archegonia
cushion of prothallus

antheridia on prothallus

small fern developing from fertilised archegonium

rhizoides

small developing fern with roots

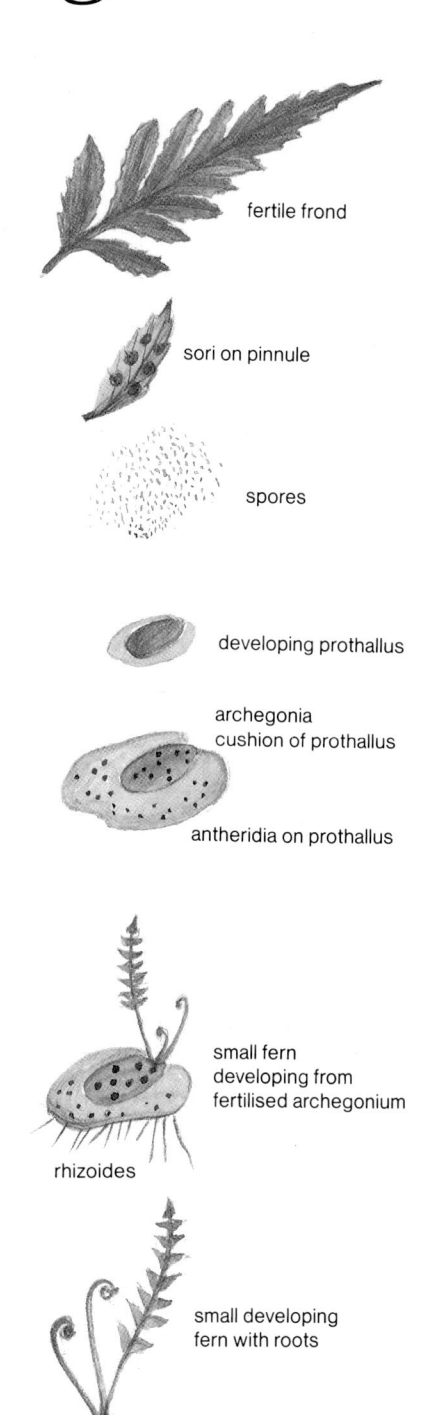

Sexual development of ferns

Successful germination of spores requires that the medium used be as sterile as possible. When the medium is contaminated various algae, fungi, liverworts and mosses develop and overgrow the developing prothalli. (Pouring boiling water over a brick, for example, does not ensure 100% sterility, but is sufficient for the exercise.)

A constant supply of water must be maintained.

Collecting Spores

When collecting the spores, a hand lens × 10 can help in determining whether the indusium, a thin layer covering the top of the sori, is open and ready to dehisce. Otherwise, tap and scrape the under surface of the fertile frond—dust-like spores will fall if they are mature. Collect the spores by placing a section of the frond inside a folded sheet of paper. If no spores appear keep the fern under observation until the spores are ripe.

In the fern allies, e.g. *Lycopodium* and *Selaginella*, the spores are produced in the axils of specialised sporophyll leaves and a number are congregated together to form cones or strobili. These spores are either male or female which under suitable conditions germinate into male or female prothalli. The sperm from the male prothalli swim through a film of moisture to the female prothalli, bringing about fertilisation. Collect the cones when they are turning brown; again, a hand lens × 10 will help to determine whether the sporangia are open and exposing the spores. Collect the spores between folded paper.

GERMINATING SPORES

Spores may be placed on any sterilised material which holds moisture—a brick, a terracotta pot, coarse sand and peat moss, fern fibre or peat moss—and kept in a saturated atmosphere inside a clear plastic bag with a small amount of boiled water.

Propagation by the following method allows for easy handling.

Make a mixture of equal parts of peat moss and coarse river sand or perlite. Sterilise in an oven at 100°C, or boil for 30 minutes.

Soak a seed punnet and plastic ice-cream container in a strong chlorine solution for 20 minutes and then wash in boiled water. Fill the punnet with the medium and soak in boiled water until thoroughly saturated.

Sprinkle the spores over the surface and place the punnet in the plastic container with about 1 cm water in the base. Enclose it all in a clear plastic bag and tie at the top. Keep in a well lighted position but not in the sun.

Within a few weeks a green moss-like film should form on the medium if the spores are fertile; after a few months the prothalli will develop. Eventually small fern fronds will develop from the prothalli. At this stage the tiny plants may be sprayed with a weak solution of liquid fertiliser.

As the fronds develop the small plants may be transplanted into community punnets filled with a mixture of peat moss, leaf mould and coarse river sand. Water well and spray with a weak solution of liquid fertiliser before enclosing in a clear plastic bag tied at the top. A little moisture on the inside of the bag will help maintain a saturated atmosphere. Still keep away from the sun, but in a well lighted position.

Open the bag for short intervals as the plants begin to grow, gradually extending the time each day until the bag can be dispensed with altogether. Water daily and fertilise monthly.

As the plants grow larger, transplant them into 50 mm pots using the same mixture. As the ferns develop they can be transplanted into larger containers.

A simple rule to remember is that most ferns do not like sun between 9 am and 5 pm.

Ferns are subject to attack by snails, slugs, grasshoppers and the chewing larvae of various insects. These must be kept under control by using snail bait or spraying with Malathion.

VEGETATIVE PROPAGATION

With few exceptions, e.g. single crown ferns, ferns can be multiplied by division of sections.
1. Ferns with multiple crowns, e.g. *Polystichum*, can be divided into separate plants.
2. Ferns with short or long creeping branched stems or rhizomes, above or below ground, can be divided into a number of plants.
3. Some ferns produce small growths which develop into small ferns, e.g. *Asplenium*.
4. Some ferns develop small plants on the body of the fern which may be removed and grown on as separate plants, e.g. *Platycerium*.
5. Some ferns have fleshy ear-like projections which can be removed and grown on into new plants.
6. Water ferns with rhizomes can be divided. Some can be broken into small pieces which will develop into separate plants.
7. Fern allies can be divided.

Soil Mix

For vegetative propagation of ferns use a mixture of equal proportions of peat moss, sphagnum moss, leaf mould, small pieces of charcoal, coarse river sand or perlite.

For fern allies use sphagnum moss.

Propagating Methods

The use of a glasshouse with bottom heat can speed up the development of divided fern sections. A cutting frame (see page 69) is also ideal to provide the necessary humid conditions.

To assist root formation water the divided sections with a small quantity of Hormone 20 added. Continual watering is essential. Keep the plants in a well lighted position out of direct sunlight.

Divisions should be made when plants are in active growth, using a sharp knife to cut apart the sections.

Tree Ferns

Cyathea and *Dicksonia* do not form branches from the stem, but occasionally small plants from spores will develop along the stem. These plants can be cut off and grown on in a container filled with soil mix. Water with a Hormone 20 solution and fertilise with a liquid fertiliser. Water daily and more frequently during hot, dry weather.

The stem of *Dicksonia* can be cut below the crown with sufficient length to be planted in a large container to a depth of about 30 cm, using soil mix. Water regularly and fertilise every month until sufficient roots have developed before planting into the ground—this could take twelve months or more. As it can take two years before these ferns become established, constant care is still required. No growth develops from the base of the cut off fern, which dies, so this method has very limited application.

With the species *Cyathea* it may be two or three years before sufficient roots develop to support the crown of the cut off section. Some species never form sufficient roots for survival.

Ferns with Multiple Crowns

Doodia, Polystichum, Christella, some species of *Asplenium*: Using a sharp knife divide the plants into separate crowns, leaving them in situ and watering well with a Hormone 20 solution and fertilising monthly with a liquid fertiliser.

After three months the divided crowns may be lifted, potted on into soil mix (page 107) and grown on until they are well established. Do not neglect watering.

point of division of extended rhizome

point of division of crown

Doodia aspera

Ferns with Creeping Underground Rhizomes

Adiantum, Lindsaea, Histiopteris, Hypolepis, Pellaea, Pteris, Nephrolepis (this genus also produces bulb-like growths along the rhizome): Cut new growth sections of the rhizome with one or two new fronds from the plant and pot into soil mix (page 107). It may take two to six months for the new growth to become well established.

With *Nephrolepis* ensure that a bulb-like growth is still attached to the section of rhizome, as this assists in establishment.

With ferns such as Psilotum, cut a section of the rhizome with a growing apex and one or two fronds, place in sphagnum moss until rooted. Pot on (plant and sphagnum moss) into a container filled with soil mix (page 107). Water with Hormone 20 solution and fertilise with a liquid fertiliser. These plants may take many months to establish.

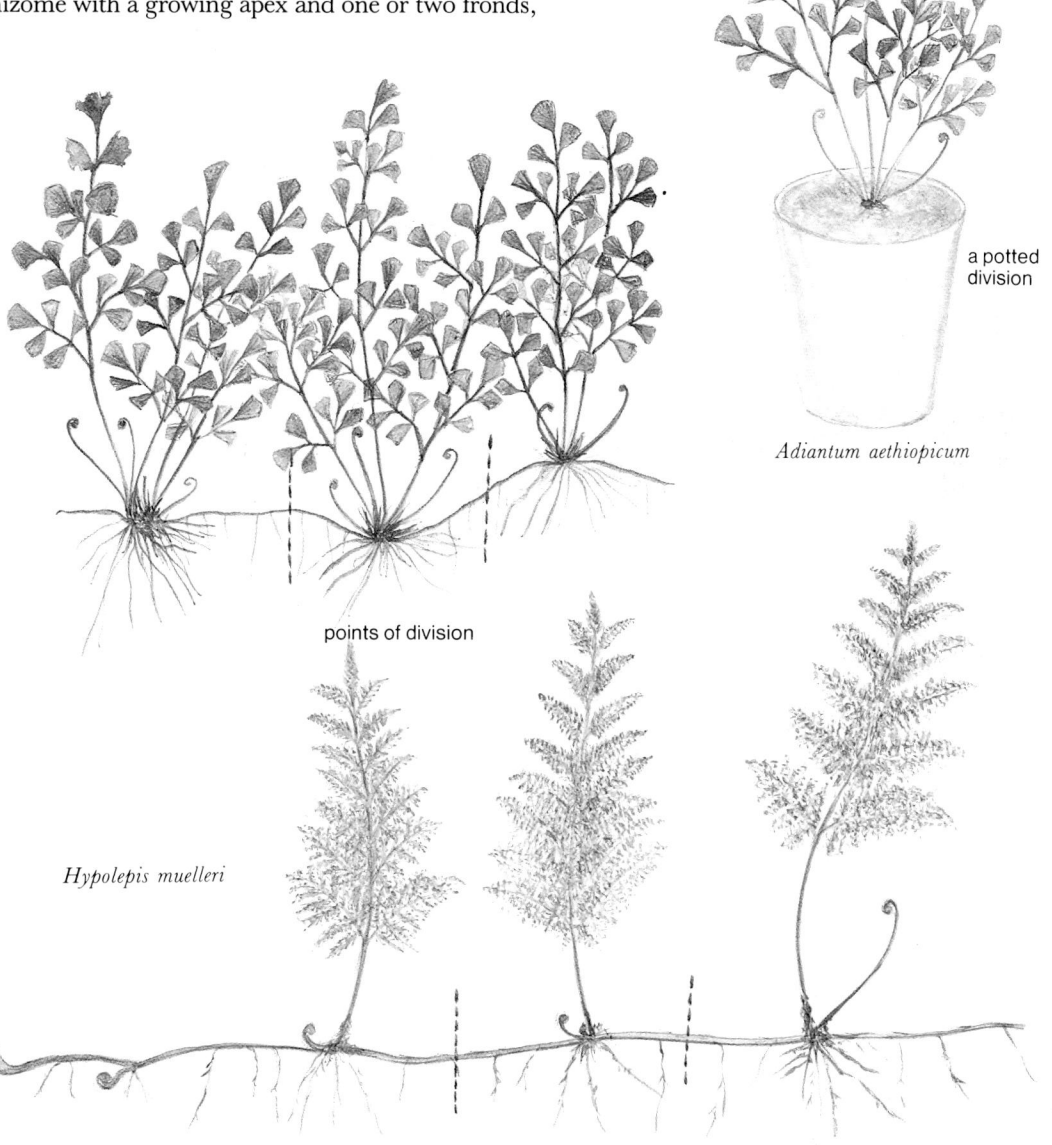

a potted division

Adiantum aethiopicum

points of division

Hypolepis muelleri

points of rhizome division

Ferns with Creeping Rhizomes Above the Ground

Microsorium, Davallia, Rumohra, Pyrrosia: These ferns creep over the stems of trees and rocks and usually grow in rainforest conditions.

Cut new growing rhizome branches from the plant and peg them down in a container filled with soil mix (page 107). Grow on as described on page 107 until established.

Strongly growing plants may be kept as potted plants, e.g. in fern baskets, or tied to a suitable surface. *Pyrrosia*, which grows on bark or rock surfaces, should be severed and attached by tying to similar surfaces.

Constant watering is needed in all cases.

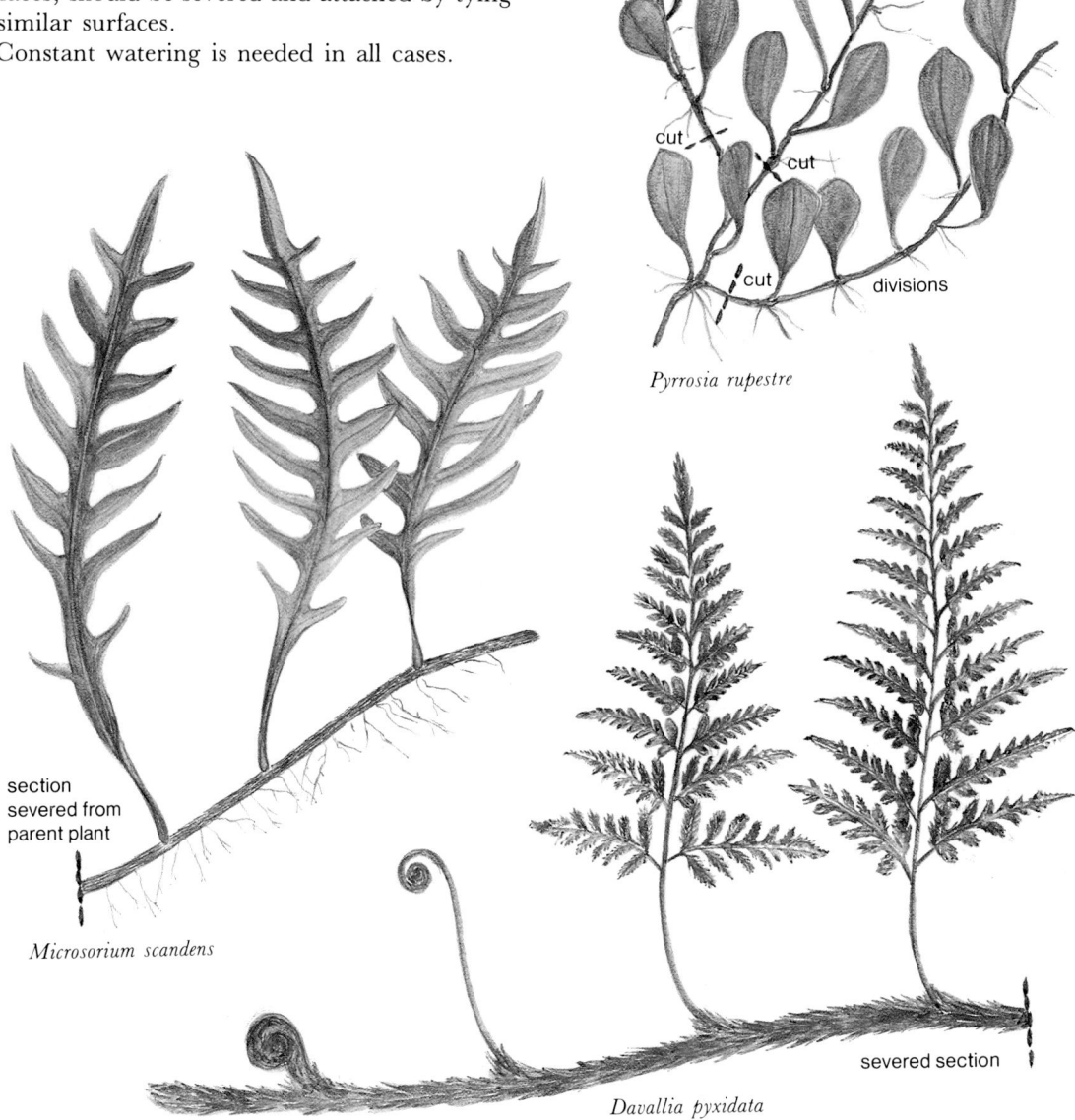

Pyrrosia rupestre

Microsorium scandens

Davallia pyxidata

FERNS WHICH PRODUCE SMALL PLANTS ON THE FRONDS

Polystichum, Asplenium: These ferns, known as Hen and Chicken Ferns, form small ferns (bulbils) on the fronds. Allow the bulbils to develop to a reasonable size before pegging down into a container filled with soil mix. Water with Hormone 20 and leave in position until the roots from the small plants are well developed. Then cut away from the main frond and grow on in the normal way.

Alternatively, allow the new plants to develop on the frond until they in turn develop new fronds. Cut away 50 mm below the bulbil, plant in soil mix and grow on.

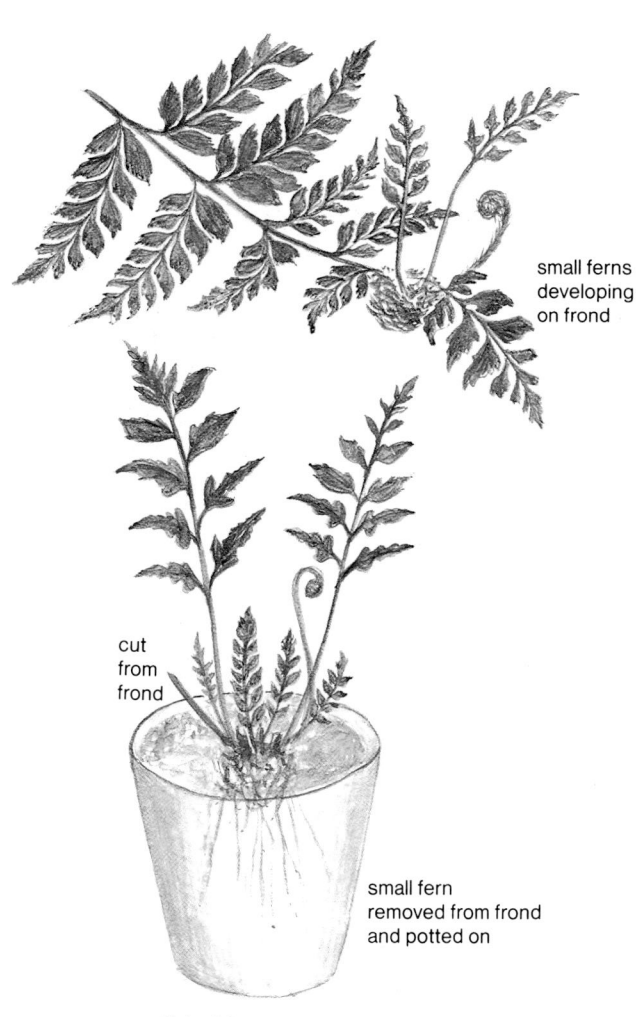

small ferns developing on frond

small fern developing on frond

cut from frond

small fern removed from frond and potted on

Polystichum proliferum

Asplenium flabellifolium

Ferns such as Elkhorns

Small plants develop on the surface of the sterile fronds. These can be cut off and attached to a suitable surface such as a tree which does not shed its bark, a terracotta pot, or a container filled with peat moss. Water with a solution of Aquasol to which a small quantity of Hormone 20 has been added. Grow in a shady position, water daily and fertilise monthly.

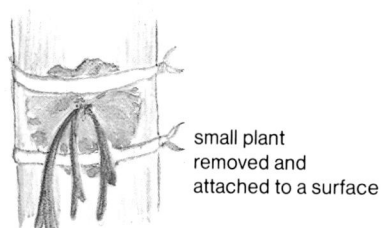

small plant developing on parent plant

small plant removed and attached to a surface

Platycerium bifurcatum

Ferns which Produce Ear-like Projections

Angiopteris and *Marattia:* These ferns are almost impossible to propagate from spores but may be reproduced vegetatively from the fleshy ear-like projections, called auricles, which are produced at the base of the frond stalk or stipe and become prominent in well developed plants which have shed old fronds.

The auricles are cut off as a wedge from the short thick trunk or rhizome. Plant with the narrow end in the soil mix and water with water containing Hormone 20 and a fertiliser. Keep in a glasshouse or cutting frame (page 69). The use of bottom heat can speed up the development of a small fern from the auricle.

Development is very slow; it may be twelve months or more before a small frond and sufficient roots develop to support the plant.

When the auricle has developed into a small fern transfer it to a moist bush-house. Water regularly.

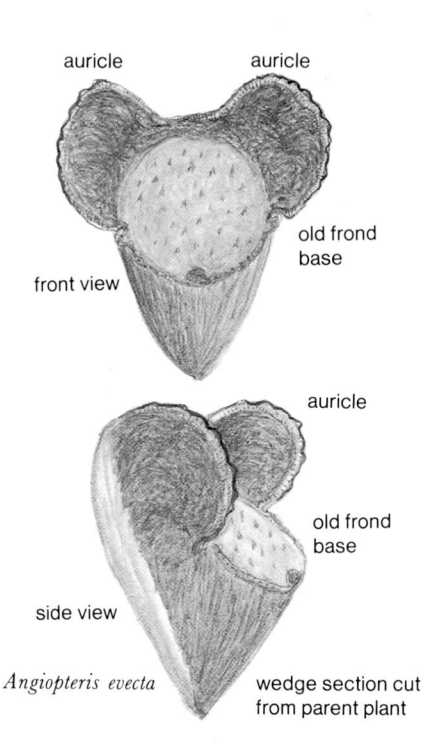

auricle auricle

front view

old frond base

auricle

side view

old frond base

Angiopteris evecta

wedge section cut from parent plant

FERN ALLIES

Lycopodium and *Selaginella:* The Clubmosses, *Lycopodium*, include both terrestrial and epiphytic species.

The rhizome of the terrestrial species is often deep in the ground. Cut a section with growing apex and several stems, plant in soil mix and treat as outlined on page 107. These plants can take twelve months or more to establish.

The Tassel Ferns, which are epiphytic, develop roots on the mature pendulous stems which turn up at the ends when they come in contact with a moist surface. By pegging the lower part of the stems back to sphagnum moss, roots can be induced to form. When this occurs cut off the section, place in a tray of sphagnum moss and allow to grow as a separate plant. Alternatively the end of the stem may be cut off and placed in sphagnum moss.

Water freely and grow in a glasshouse.

Selaginella species usually creep over the surface of moist areas and produce numerous side branches. These can be pegged down on a tray of sphagnum moss; when well rooted sever from the parent plant and transplant (plant and sphagnum moss) to the surface of a container filled with soil mix (page 107).

Water freely.

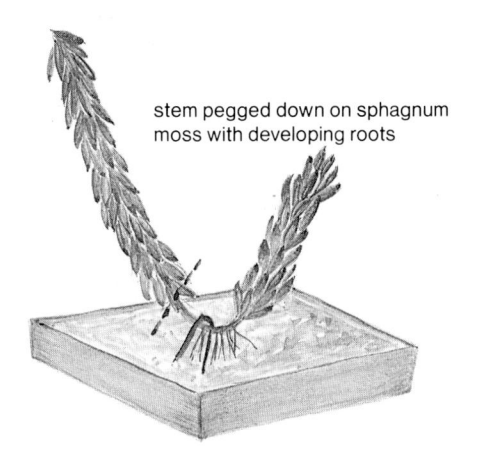

Lycopodium squarrosum

stem pegged down on sphagnum moss with developing roots

WATER FERNS

Marsillea and *Azolla: Marsillea* ferns increase by branching rhizomes which usually grow under water, but often creep into moist soils. They are readily propagated by cutting sections of the outer growing rhizomes and transplanting to waterproof containers with a small amount of silty soil in the base. Fill the container with water. They can also be planted in shallow pools where the four-lobed leaves will float on the surface.

Small floating ferns, e.g. *Azolla*, may be broken into small sections and transferred to other water containers—each section will develop into a separate plant.

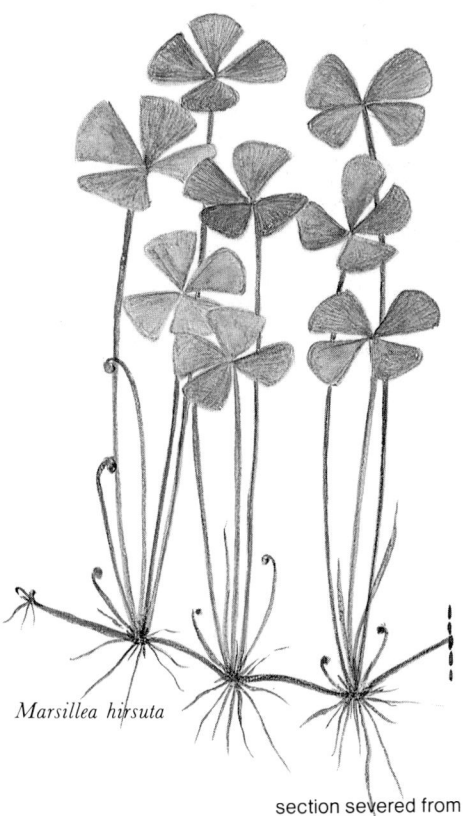

Marsillea hirsuta

section severed from parent plant

Appendix – Planting Out

Before seedlings and cuttings are planted out they should be allowed to develop a good root system. To check this, water the plant well and allow it to drain, then remove the plant from the pot and assess that sufficient roots have developed. If there are no obvious roots, return the plant to the container and allow it to grow on for a further period until more roots have developed.

hole dug and checked for size with plant in container

hole filled with water and allowed to drain away

plant in container immersed in a bucket of water

Prior to planting, harden the plant to the conditions under which it is to grow by removing it from the protection of a bush-house and growing in the open for about two weeks. During this time water regularly.

Most plants require a well drained soil for success. The problem of poor drainage can be readily overcome in most gardens by the use of agricultural drains and raised garden beds. If this is not practical or possible badly drained areas should be avoided except for moisture loving species such as Callistemons and Melaleucas which can tolerate badly drained soil.

The best time for planting out is generally early autumn, except in areas subject to heavy frost where early spring is preferable. Summer planting should be avoided.

Dig a hole slightly larger than the container in which the plant is growing. To test the size of the hole try the potted plant for size, filling in or removing soil if required, so the surface of the plant soil is just level with or slightly below the soil level.

Avoid digging deeply into a clay base on heavier soils as this causes pondage when the plant is watered and could cause root rot.

Fill the hole with water and allow to drain away (repeat if the soil is very dry). At the same time soak the plant in a bucket of water until air bubbles cease to rise from the soil. Remove the pot and drain.

Upend the pot to remove the plant from the container, and carefully tease out the roots before placing it in position in the hole, ensuring that the plant soil surface is level with or slightly lower than the surrounding ground.

Fill in around the plant, making sure there are no air spaces, and build shallow shoulders in a circle around the plant to help in directing water to it. Finally, water the plant thoroughly.

While the plant is establishing itself in its new position water well each week for about three months, then monthly for about another year.

plant drained and removed from container and roots gently teased out

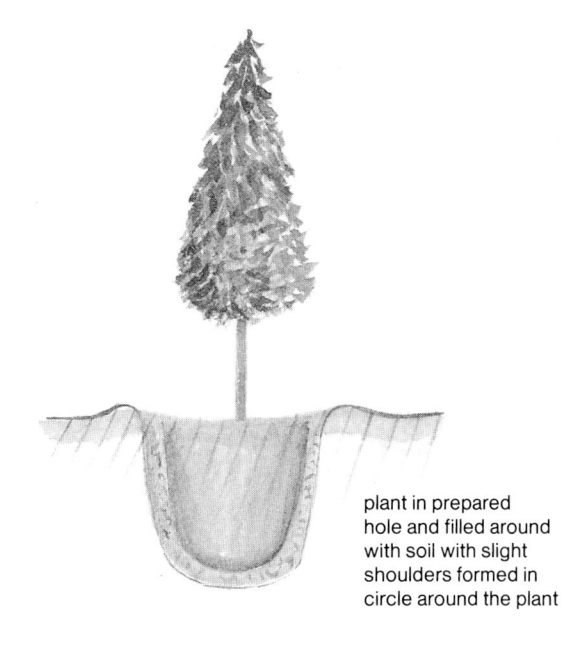

plant in prepared hole and filled around with soil with slight shoulders formed in circle around the plant

Glossary

Page numbers refer to illustrations

Achene   a one-seeded dry fruit which does not open when ripe (indehiscent), formed from a superior ovary of one carpel and free of the carpel or case (pages 27, 34)
Adventitious   produced in an unusual position, e.g. a shoot rising from a root, buds arising from the stem at places other than from a leaf axil
Algae   a group of simple plants with chlorophyll, formed from a single cell or with multiple single cells such as in seaweed (page 6)
Angiosperm   flowering plant which produces its seed in an ovary, unlike a gymnosperm which produces its seed on the surface of a scale
Annual   a plant that germinates from seed, flowers and dies in one year
Anther   that part of the stamen which contains the pollen (pages 22, 26)
Antheridium   an organ of the sexual stage of spore bearing plants which produces the male cells and may be likened to the anther in seed bearing plants, plural *antheridia* (page 105)
Archegonium   an organ of the sexual stage of spore bearing plants which produces the female cells and may be likened to the ovule of seed bearing plants; the female sexual stage of Bryophytes, pteridophytes, conifers and cycads, plural *archegonia* (page 105)
Auricle   an ear-like appendage at the base of a leaf; it may be thin and mebraneous, as in *Freycinetia*, or thick and fleshy, as in the auricles at the base of the fronds in the ferns *Angiopteris* and *Marattia* where they are arranged as stipules (page 112)
Aril   a fleshy appendage covering all or part of the testa of a seed, formed from the funicle
Auxin   a natural or synthetic substance regulating the growth of plants (hormone)
Axil   the point or angle between the stem and the leaf (page 21)
Axis   the long stem-like support on which plant organs are arranged, e.g. the central stem of an inflorescence
Biennial   a plant that flowers and dies in the second year.

Berry   a fleshy fruit with the seeds embedded in the pulp (pages 27, 37)
Bract   a modified leaf that subtends (i.e., embraces or encloses) in its axil a flower or an inflorescence
Bracteole   a small bract or appendage usually occurring in pairs on a flower, pedicel or calyx (page 22)
Bryophytes   a group of simple plants with chlorophyll, which includes liverworts and mosses (page 6)
Bulb   a short underground stem with overlapping scales in which plant foods are stored and from which a stem, leaves and flowers develop (page 19)
Callus   a growth of tissue arising from the cambium which protects damaged plant surfaces such as in a cutting; the particular cells are known as parenchyma
Calyx   the outer ring of floral leaves, each segment of which is known as a sepal (page 22)
Capsule   a dry fruit of two or more united carpels which open when ripe (pages 27, 38–42)
Cambium   the group of meristem cells between the phloem and xylem from which develop new growth cells (page 13)
Cambium layer   the outer growth ring of tissue formed in dicotyledenous plants which form new rings of wood (page 13)
Carpel   the organ of the female part of the flower in which one or more ovules are produced (see *ovary*) with a stigma and sometimes a style (page 22)
Cell   the basic unit of plant structure
Chlorophyll   the green pigment of plants which absorbs light energy in the process of photosynthesis
Coccus   see *Mericarp*; plural *cocci* (page 52)
Coralloid roots   specialised roots which develop in Cycads and grow upward to near the ground surface; these roots contain a blue-green algae which is believed to form a symbiotic relationship with the host plant (page 10)
Cone   a group of sporophylls more or less compactly arranged around a central axis as in conifers and cycads; loosely used for multiple fruit arranged around a central axis, e.g. Casuarinaceae, *Petrophile* and *Banksia* (page 9)
Corm   a fleshy swollen underground stem in which

reserve food is stored and which produces aerial stems, leaves and flowers (page 19)

Cortex the tissue on the outer side of and surrounding the phloem in stems and roots of dicotyledonous plants (page 13)

Cotyledon a seed leaf of the embryo of a seed plant (page 28)

Cross pollination the transfer of the pollen from the anther of one plant to the stigma of another plant (pages 25, 26)

Cypsela (achene) a dry indehiscent one-seeded fruit formed from an inferior ovary which occurs in most daisies (Asteraceae) and is often surmounted by a pappus (pages 27, 34)

Deciduous falling off, as with leaves, and petals after flowering

Dehiscent opening or bursting when ripe as in anthers and fruit

Dicotyledon a plant in which the seed embryo has two cotyledons (page 62)

Drupe a succulent indehiscent fruit with an outer skin and a middle fleshy layer overlying a hard stony layer enclosing the seed (pages 27, 43)

Embryo the young plant in the rudimentary stage in a mature seed, or in a fertilised archegonium after development

Endosperm the nutrient substance surrounding the embryo in some seeds

Epicotyl the section above the cotyledon, the axis of the plumule

Epiphyte a plant lodged or attached, but not parasitic, on another plant or surface

Evergreen a plant bearing leaves throughout the year

Fertile capable of reproducing itself: of flowers, producing seed; of anthers, containing pollen; of ferns, antheridia containing sperms, archegonia containing egg cells; of conifers and cycads, sporophylls containing microspores or pollen or with ovules

Fertilisation in flowering plants, the union of pollen with an ovule to form a seed; of ferns, the union of a sperm from an antheridium with an egg cell in an archegonium to form a small plant; of conifers and cycads, the union of a microspore with an ovule to form seed

Follicle a dry one-celled fruit consisting of a single carpel that splits and opens along the line of fusion of the two edges (pages 27, 44–47, 51)

Fruit the mature ovary and whatever part of the flower that may be attached to it at the time the seed is ripe; the seed bearing structure of flowering plants

Fungus a thallophytic plant which has no chlorophyll and reproduces by spores produced in fruiting bodies of various forms; plural *fungi* (page 6)

Funicle the stalk attaching the ovule to the ovary (page 55)

Gamete a reproductive cell which unites with another in sexual reproduction

Gametophyte the organ which bears the sexual gamete

Genus a group of closely related species; can be a single species with no other closely related species

Gymnosperm non-flowering plants in which the seed is naked, i.e. not enclosed in an ovary, and is carried on the surface of a scale (sporophyll)

Herbaceous a green, more or less soft type of plant; applied to parts of the plant which are green and soft in texture

Heterosporous producing two types of spores in mega- and micro-gametophytes

Hirsute having a covering of coarse stiff longish hairs

Hybrid the progeny of two different plant species

Hypocotyl the embryonic stem below the cotyledon (page 28)

Indehiscent not splitting or opening when ripe

Inferior ovary an ovary situated below the calyx (page 22)

Internode the plant stem between the nodes (page 13)

Keikis aerial plants which develop from buds or sometimes inflorescences as in *Dendrobium* and *Sarcochilus*. These plants form leaves and roots, may flower or form new growth from their bases (page 94)

Labellum the third petal of the flower in orchid species which differs from other petals; the fifth or smallest petal in the Stylidiaceae family (page 22)

Legume or pod a folded carpel which splits down both edges when ripe (pages 27, 48–50)

Lignotuber a woody often conspicuous swelling at the base of the stem which as well as storing food has dormant buds from which new shoots arise (page 13)

Medullary ray bands of tissue radiating from the bark to the pith in dicotyledonous plants which assist in transporting plant foods and oxygen (page 13)

Megasporangium the megaspore sporangium in which megaspores develop

Megaspore the large female spore of heterosporous plants

Mericarp a single segment of a fruit, a carpel which separates at maturity from a schizocarp; a carpel containing one seed; also called a coccus (page 52)

Micropyle an opening in an ovule allowing fertilisation to occur which also allows the radicle to emerge in germination

Microspore the small male spore or pollen of heterosporous plants

Microsporangium a sporangium which produces microspores as in heterosporous plants

Monocotyledon flowering plants whose seed embryo usually has one seed leaf (page 23)

Mycorrhiza the association of special groups of fungi which grow around the surface of the roots (ectotrophic), or within the tissue of the roots (endotrophic), of many plants in a symbiotic relationship, the fungi providing water, nitrogen and mineral substances to and receiving carbohydrates from the plant (page 10)

Node that part of the stem, often enlarged, at which the leaves arise and in the axil of which new shoots arise (page 13)

Nut a one-celled fruit which contains one seed, which does not open when ripe and is formed from two or more carpels (pages 27, 51)

Ovary the basal portion of the pistil formed from one or a group of carpels which enclose the ovule or ovules (page 22)

Ovule a structure in a seed plant within which one or more megaspores are formed, which after fertilisation develops into a seed; the megaspore of seed plants; an immature seed

Parenchyma the soft non-woody tissue of plants; the tissues deposited to repair damaged areas, e.g. the callus which forms on the cut surface of a cutting

Perennial a plant whose life cycle extends beyond two growing seasons; a plant living for a number of years

Perianth floral leaves, calyx and petals collectively, particularly when they are similar (page 25)

Petiole the stalk of a leaf (page 21)

Phloem the tissues on the outer side of the cambium cells which conduct dissolved plant food substances from the leaves (page 13)

Pith the soft spongy tissue in the middle of stems and roots of dicotyledonous plants; formed of parenchyma cells

Phyllode a flattened or modified petiole serving the function of a leaf (page 21)

Pinna a leaflet; the primary division of a pinnate leaf; plural *pinnae*

Pinnule the secondary pinna in a bipinnate leaf (page 21)

Pistil the female part of the flower, usually consisting of a stigma, a stalk or style and an ovary (page 22)

Plumule the embryo shoot of a seed (page 28)

Pod or legume a folded carpel which splits down both sides when ripe (pages 27, 48–50)

Pollen the dust-like grains or microspores contained in an anther; the microspore of seed plants (page 26)

Pollen tube the tube which develops from a germinating pollen grain and grows through the stigma to the ovule in the ovary to bring about fertilisation (page 26)

Pollination the transfer of pollen to the stigma; the transfer of microspores to the pollen chamber of conifers and cycads (page 26)

Pollinium a group of waxy pollen grains adhering together in Orchidaceae and Asclepiadaceae families (page 26)

Proteoid roots specialised roots which develop in many species of the family Proteaceae, whose function is to absorb the low phosphorus levels in Australian soils; these roots live for about three months but are regularly replaced (page 10)

Prothallus a gametophyte of ferns and fern allies which develops from the germination of a spore (pages 24, 105)

Pseudobulb in orchids more correctly applied to those species which have swollen bulb-like enlargements at the base of leaves as in *Calanthe*, *Phaius* and *Cymbidium*; wrongly applied to orchids such as *Dendrobium* which have fleshy stems (pages 94, 95, 97, 102)

Radicle the embryo root of seed plants (page 28)

Rhizoid root-like growths which develop from the body of simple plants such as liverworts and mosses and from the prothallus of ferns which attach the plant to the surface on which they are growing (pages 6, 24)

Rhizobia a genus of bacteria which penetrate the root hairs and enter the root cells of leguminous plants forming nodules which fix nitrogen for the plant

Rhizome a creeping, usually underground, stem; commonly growing on a surface above the ground in epiphytic plants such as orchids and ferns (page 13)

Samara a winged fruit, the wing being formed from the walls of the fruit, as in Casuarinaceae (page 54)

Schizocarp a dry fruit which when mature divides into several one-seeded carpels, each carpel known as a mericarp or a coccus (pages 27, 52)

Seed the fertilised mature ovule which contains the embryo

Shoot a young growing branch or twig

Species a unit of classification for an individual or population of individuals which have common features and are capable of interbreeding and producing the same characteristics

Sporangium the sac or receptacle within which spores are produced

Sporophyll a specialised spore-bearing leaf-like organ on which one or more sporangia are borne (page 9)

Stamen part of a flower with an anther which produces pollen and usually consists of an anther and a stalk or filament (page 22)

Stem the main part or axis system of a plant developed from the embryo plumule (page 13)

Sterile infertile and unable to reproduce

Stigma the female part of the plant which is receptive to pollen; usually at the apex of the style (pages 22, 26)

Stipe a stalk of a superior ovary; the petiole of a fern (page 22)

Strobilus a cone, bearing sporangia, as in *Lycopodium*

Style that part of the pistil between the stigma and the ovary (page 22)

Superior ovary an ovary situated above the floral parts (page 22)

Symbiosis two organisms living together with mutual benefit to each other, e.g. mycorrhizal fungi on the roots of plants

Thallophytes a group of simple plants which have a simple body such as algae, fungi, liverworts and mosses (page 6)

Thallus a simple plant body which does not form separate roots, stem and leaves, as in thallophytes

Tuber a swollen underground stem which acts as a reservoir of stored food and has buds capable of producing new stems and leaves, e.g. potato (page 19)

Tuberoid a small tuber produced by many terrestrial orchids (page 19)

Vascular bundle the elongated strands of tissue in groups of special cells forming vessels of conducting cells in higher plants (page 13)

Vascular tissue plant tissue consisting of ducts or vessels in higher plants which form the system by which sap is conveyed through the plant

Xylem the woody part of vascular bundles on the inner side of the cambium cells which are specialised for the conduction of water, nitrogen and dissolved mineral substances (page 13)

BIBLIOGRAPHY

Blombery, A.M. (1977) *Australian Native Plants*, Angus & Robertson, Sydney

—— (1984) *Practical Gardening and Landscaping with Australian Native Plants,* Angus & Robertson, Sydney

Blombery, A.M. and Maloney, B.F. (1981) *Proteaceae of the Sydney Region,* Angus & Robertson, Sydney

—— (1992) *The Proteaceae of the Sydney Region*, Kangaroo Press, Sydney

Bowen, A.T.M. (1965) *Introduction to Botany*, Newnes, London

Brewster, A.A. and Le Plastrier, C.M. (*c.* 1922) *Botany for Australian Students*, Radcliffe Press, Sydney

George, A.S. Executive Editor (1981) *Flora of Australia*, Vol. 1, Australian Government Publishing Service, Canberra

Harden, G.J. Editor (1990–1991) *Flora of New South Wales*, Vols 1 and 2, New South Wales University Press, Sydney

Hartmann, H.T., Kester, D.E. and Davies Jr, F.T. (1990) *Plant Propagation: Principles and Practices*, 5th ed., Prentice Hall, New Jersey

Jones, D.L. and Clemesha, S.C. (1984) *Australian Ferns and Fern Allies*, Reed Books, Sydney

Kelly, N., Hatherly, J. and Rosen, G. (1987) *Focus on Life*, McGraw-Hill, Sydney

Leach, J.A. (1922) *Australian Nature Studies*, Critchley Parker, Melbourne

McLuckie, J. and McKee, H.S. (1962) *Australian and New Zealand Botany*, Horwitz and Grahams, Sydney

Stover, E.L. (1951) *Anatomy of Seed Plants*, Heath D.C., Boston